The Impact
of
Mass Media

HAYDEN ENGLISH LANGUAGE SERIES

Robert W. Boynton — Consulting Editor

*Former Principal, Senior High School
and Chairman, English Department
Germantown Friends School*

The Impact of Mass Media

PEARL G. ALDRICH

Frostburg State College
Frostburg, Maryland

HAYDEN BOOK COMPANY, INC.
Rochelle Park, New Jersey

for
HARVEY, who operated
LOUISE, who sustained
and
LUCILLE, who tiptoed around
the typewriter when I got stuck

Permissions

Excerpt from "Welcome to the Consumption Community" from *The Decline of Radicalism* by Daniel J. Boorstin, reprinted by permission of Random House, Inc.

Excerpt from the Preamble of *The Television Code*, reprinted by permission of the Code Authority, National Association of Broadcasters.

Newspaper article, "Kid Journalists Are Confronting Freebies, Surviving," reprinted by permission of the Knight Newspapers.

Paragraph from "Great Change-overs for You" by Marshall McLuhan, reprinted by permission of the author.

Excerpt from *Television: The Business Behind the Box* by Les Brown, reprinted by permission of Harcourt Brace Jovanovich, Inc.

Excerpt from *Theories of Mass Communication* by Melvin L. DeFleur, reprinted by permission of David McKay Company, Inc.

Library of Congress Cataloging in Publication Data

Aldrich, Pearl G
     The impact of mass media.

     (Hayden English language series)
     Bibliography: p.
     1. Mass media—United States.   I.   Title.
P92.U5A4   301.16'1'0973   75-1012
ISBN 0-8104-6001-7
ISBN 0-8104-6000-9   pbk.

Printed in the United States of America

7	8	9		PRINTING
81	82	83		YEAR

Permissions (Cont'd.)

Foreword to the Student

"Why, sometimes I've believed as many as six impossible things before breakfast," the Queen tells Alice in *Through the Looking Glass*. One needs only, the Queen assures her, to practice believing the impossible for just half an hour a day.

How many impossible things in the mass media have *you* believed in the past twenty-four hours? Impossible to tell? This plain-speaking book can help you begin the process of "unbelieving." As a manual for analyzing both the media and their messages, it provides an abundance of activities that get you directly involved in assessing the seemingly endless array of words, sounds, pictures, and body language that vie for your undivided attention every waking hour. For example: How do you discover the "images" in advertising to which you are expected to respond? The book takes you behind the scenes to look at marketing techniques, then guides you to make assessments on your own.

"The main thrust of this text," the author tells us, "is to disperse the fog of confusion about the media, created both by time and deliberate effort, so that you can see your options clearly." To this end Ms. Aldrich has provided you with rather penetrating fog lights. If you keep to the road she charts, you cannot help seeing your options with considerable clarity.

Keep to the road. You will find the trip worthwhile.

ANTHONY TOVATT

Foreword to the Teacher

At the 1972 convention of the National Council of Teachers of English, the following resolution was passed:

It has been estimated that 96% of American homes now have television sets, which are in use more than six hours a day in the average home. Obviously, since most young people spend so much time with television or radio, they acquire wide-spread impressions of human life and events from these media. Be it therefore

RESOLVED,

That the NCTE go on record as favoring the teaching of television and radio evaluation in both elementary and secondary schools, and, to that end, propose that colleges and universities prepare prospective and current teachers for the task of developing in their students evaluative skills for these media.

This text is offered as a practical way to implement the resolution of the NCTE, extending such evaluative skills from the electronic medium to the print medium as well.

Because the majority of mass media texts are laudatory and the media are self-serving, we need to start educating students in ways of thoughtful analysis and provide specific means of going about it. To meet these interlocking goals, this book is slightly unorthodox in both content and presentation. Such departures from tradition grew from my own efforts to solve the problems of teaching evaluative skills in so fluid a subject as contemporary mass media.

One of the main problems to overcome is topicality. By the time a book is written and through the press, names and events are out of date. This text, therefore, does not name specific programs, personalities, news events, crises, conflicts, and other topical matters. It provides general principles by which to evaluate current media offerings and outlines the patterns from which media materials are cut for public consumption. Then it focuses the student's attention on the mass media themselves. This method has two major advantages. It brings the student's contemporary environment into the classroom for study, and it keeps the book useful from year to year.

The Advance Preparations at the beginning of each chapter are for both students and teachers, with more materials available in the Teaching Resources section at the back of the book. All these are provided to help teachers with limited background in the mass media prepare for classes without inordinate time consumption. Making telephone calls, gathering library materials, searching out records and video and oral tape recordings, and doing other necessary tasks can be distributed so that no one person's burdens will be overwhelming.

Another major problem that the design of the book tries to meet is the increasing flexibility in course length, which may range from mini-courses and phase electives of two to nine weeks to quinmesters, trimesters, and traditional semesters. This problem is handled by the number and variety of Activities which allow the book to be used like an accordian—compress it for short courses by choosing a few Activities; expand it for long courses by using more of the Activities. By choosing from among the Advance Preparations and Activities, you can make this text fit any course format from mini to maxi.

Other reasons for the large number of Activities include the following: No two classes are ever identical, nor are teachers' ideas for assignments. Special events, controversies, crises boil up, and it is vital to include them as they are happening. Differences in equipment exist from school to school. Scheduling of speakers and use of recordings and film must be left to individual situations. Therefore, use the Activities as a well-stocked smorgasbord—pick and choose.

Another departure from tradition in this text is the omission of footnotes. There are several reasons for this. The major one is that the book is highly personal. The bulk of the material, except for the history provided in the chapters on the pattern-setting days of print and electronic media, is based on my personal experience of working in the media. This experience has provided the philosophy, viewpoint, and central theme of the book. It is as personal and individual a presentation as any teacher's in his or her own classroom. As such, it is also available for support or opposition from data collected by the students. Such give and take is the way I taught the courses from which this text developed.

Another aspect of the personal viewpoint presented here is that the main thrust of the text is critical. The generally accepted assumption that three identical networks and two identical papers per area reflect the morally perfect, ethically right American Way of Life needs examination. Ideals learned from journalism books tarnish rapidly when a City Editor breaks his back, and yours, to please the public relations department of the industry with the strongest political clout in the state; when the state Governor sits on your desk for half an hour, priming sweet-young-girl reporter with charm interlarded by contradictory statements and manipulative techniques transparent to a child of two, and the Managing Editor, flanked by the Publisher, supports him. What an eye-opener public relations is, particularly when you go into television studios as part of the production team. It takes only a few weeks around a network affiliate to realize that, however idealistic junior echelons of management and production are, at the policy making level, there never really was any such thing as "public interest and convenience," only a hunger for profits. My criticisms of all these aspects of the media are clearly stated in the text.

The bibliographies for each section are eclectic, but not exhaustive. They provide a variety of viewpoints, from exposé to industry back-patting. Magazine articles praising or denigrating the media are so topical that I've listed mostly books. Older histories go into greater detail than current ones, but laudatory histories far outnumber critical works. For example, there is only one critical history of broadcasting—Erik Barnouw's three volumes—as against dozens of the type written by Sidney Head. Head praises the forces that have prevented government control of broadcasting without noting other forms of control, and contends, without noting the commercial and governmental forces lined up against them, that it has been education's own fault that colleges have lost their radio stations. This viewpoint is current in newspaper histories, too, particularly local histories, but there is no Erik Barnouw in journalism history. I wish Ben Bagdikian could be persuaded to turn his attention to the subject.

In devising the plan for this text, I had to establish some limits on the information to be provided. Had I attempted to cover all aspects of the mass media with scholarly thoroughness, I would have had to project at least twenty volumes and apologize on my deathbed for not completing my work. Therefore, I cut off the history of the print medium at the Civil War, and the electronic, around 1930, although I have commented about several aspects of contemporary developments. These cut-off dates are logical because, by each, the patterns of each medium had been established. With this historical background, students can look directly at media in their own time.

As a result of using this textbook, I hope that young people will be alerted to the main purpose of the mass media, will be able to identify the manipulative techniques directed against their emotions, and will not only develop evaluative skills, but, most of all, use them in making decisions. This book is dedicated to achieving that purpose.

PEARL G. ALDRICH

Contents

Chapter 1
Growing Up with the Media

What do you remember most about your childhood? Running through the long dewy grass of a meadow or the Saturday morning TV cartoons? Sitting in the kitchen watching your mother cook supper or sitting in the living room watching Captain Kangaroo? Which came first on Sunday morning—breakfast or the comics?

Now bring your memories up to date. What did you and your friends talk about, at least part of the time, before class? An item from a newspaper? An ad that you noticed in a magazine or a television commercial? An episode from a popular TV series? A movie? Or a new record that you heard on the radio?

If your answers parallel those of most young people, you add to the proof that mass media play a large and influential part in your life. Your answers also prove just how casually you accept the media, just as you accept the house you live in, cars, electricity, telephones, your school, and your family as part of your environment. Parents, teachers, church and synagogue leaders agree that all young people growing up with the media learn from them, sometimes more than adults wish you to.

If the use of *them* referring to *media* in the last sentence seems strange, remember that the word *media* linguistically is plural. When people criticize *the media* as a bad influence, they usually are talking about television, the most powerful *medium* of all. Maybe calling television *the media* can be justified technically because, as a *medium*, it embraces functions of several *media* such as newspapers, magazines, movies, and recordings. However,

1

considering that language changes are brought about by just such confusions in usage, it might not be long before educated people will accept *the media* as singular. Such linguistic changes are supposed to need about 75 to 100 years to become solid in the language, with verbal usage preceding written. In this book, however, *media* will be used as the plural and *medium* as the singular.

The major media can be divided into two kinds, print and electronic. The print media—newspapers, magazines, books, pamphlets, catalogs, circulars, brochures, anything you read—are the oldest, dating back to the invention of the printing press in the fifteenth century. The electronic media—radio, television, films of all kinds, records, tapes, anything that is transmitted by the use of electricity—are less than a hundred years old.

The word *mass*, as in *mass media*, means an extremely large number of people, the millions who are reached by the various media, either one at a time or by two or more simultaneously. One of the problems facing us today is being reached by the media when we really don't choose to be. Do you sometimes find it difficult to locate a moment of complete silence in your environment or a time when your eyes are not presented with signs, billboards, or pictures demanding attention?

Another meaning the word *mass* suggests is "the people," a phrase too often associated with adjectives like dull-witted, credulous, ill-informed, uncritical, and passive. Or are the *mass* of people well-informed, sophisticated, thoughtful, and active? Which are you? How much of what you know about yourself has been taught you by the media? You may not realize how greatly the media influence you because in your lifetime they have always been there. In fact, short of deliberate isolation on a mountain top or being lost in a forest and reared by wolves, no one will ever again grow up without the presence and influence of the mass media.

Is this good or bad?

An experiment recently conducted in Europe by the Society for Rational Psychology showed that watching television is psychologically addictive. Of 184 constant viewers paid to give up watching for one year, not one lasted more than five months because of "withdrawal symptoms." Tension, quarrelling, and physical aggression increased in families whose conflicts had been covered over by habitual viewing.

The idea of becoming addicted to television brings up questions involving subtle conditioning and brainwashing that could be friendly or vicious, altruistic or self-serving. In politics, the worst of the media's ability to create belief is persuading us to willingly elect charlatans to important public office. The best is probably politicians' inability to hide their methods, such as the revelation of the tactics used in the House Un-American Activities Committee hearings when they were televised in the 1950s, leading to Senator Joseph McCarthy's loss of power.

In a commercial society such as ours, the media's ability to stimulate motivation to buy—almost as though people were puppets on strings—builds other people's power. It can be power for good or power for bad, but it is *always* power for control. The comfort and convenience of finding the same nationally advertised merchandise wherever you live or travel must be considered against limitations of choice, shoddy manufacture, and artificially inflated and maintained prices. Intertwining monopolies in giant corporations with power in the hands of a few people, through advertising, lobbying associations, and pressure on Congress that prevents any legal accountability being applied to their actions, can eventually control your life. They certainly control the media.

All these negative aspects of growing up with the media need consideration at the same time you are enjoying the positive aspects of immediately knowing what's going on in the world, sharing great entertainment and historical events with everyone else in our "global village," and having the fun of trying out a new product that you wouldn't have known about without advertising.

According to a recent research report, more than a third of all children by the age of three are viewing TV with some regularity and more than half are listening to books read to them. Before they are old enough for school, a third of the children are looking through magazines, 40 percent are listening to radio, and 80 percent are viewing television. At age seven, newspapers enter a child's life, usually through the comic strips. You are one of these children. As you grew, you absorbed, and you absorbed uncritically, as children do.

And what did you absorb? Hundreds of items of information, most of them accurate *as far as they went.* Increasing sophistication of taste and appreciation of technical skills. High standards of performance by talented musicians and actors that sometimes make your teachers despair of competing effectively for your attention.

With all this, you also absorbed ideas about behavior, about right and wrong, good and bad, the permissible and the forbidden. These ideas were presented to you—and still are—directly and indirectly with the entertainment, advertising, and information. The most powerful ideas are the ones you absorb indirectly. They are digested emotionally at psychological depths that we still know little about, although we can tell that the effect of reaching those depths is particularly strong and long lasting from behavior patterns that emerge.

Test your own absorption pattern by answering honestly the following set of questions:

For girls—What cosmetic, hair style, dress, or bathing suit did you try to convince your mother was appropriate for you by pointing out the magazine or newspaper advertisement or TV commercial?

For boys—What piece of automotive or sports equipment did you try to get your parents to finance by the same technique?

Or, if either of you used an old-fashioned and well-known method of persuasion such as "Sue's/Joe's parents let her/him!," chances are that Sue/Joe is the one who saw or heard it in the media.

Now try this set of questions:

For boys—What brand of cake mix did you buy last?

For girls—Which brand of automobile tires did you buy?

What was that you said, Bill Jones? You don't buy things like that? You don't even notice those commercials? Clever of the media people to reflect so well current themes of men's and women's "normal" interests, isn't it? Yet, sometimes even the media people get themselves into deep wells they have difficulty climbing out of. Take men's cosmetics, for example. Only girls use cosmetics. Right? It isn't "masculine" for boys to use cosmetics. Right? Yet hair spray and cologne, the latter under the name of "after-shave lotion," are being strenuously advertised by the use of "masculine" descriptive words and pictures of athletic young men spraying their hair.

Is the fact that men's cosmetics have become the biggest selling items in stores today evidence of a positive aspect of the media—helping cultural change—or is it evidence of "creating a market" to sell more merchandise that may or may not be worthwhile?

At the same time that advertising is based upon the underlying assumption that men don't buy products aimed toward women, it also uses the idea that it is perfectly "natural" for women to buy men's products. There is an obvious advantage to the advertiser and media of playing both ends against the middle. They sell to all.

Another indication of media influence is in the language we use. Whole new vocabularies come into existence with new inventions. Look back at the first two paragraphs of this chapter. How many expressions can you identify that came into popular usage with the development of a medium? How about *TV cartoons?* Or the abbreviated version of the word *television?* In this country, we say *TV* and spell it several different ways: tv, T.V., TV, teevee. In Britain, it's the *telly,* as everyone who watches the British "stand-up" comedians will know. That term, *stand-up comic,* seems to be another media invention. Actually, a comedian does sit sometimes, whenever the action of a skit demands, but there is always that string of jokes, or would-be jokes, delivered standing up, first at a stationary microphone during early radio days, now just standing or wandering about a stage, mike in hand. In advertising, the stand-up commercial was the first kind used. In this, the announcer or star of the program would grasp the product firmly in hand, making sure the name faced the camera, and as persuasively as possible, recite or read the copy written about it at an advertising agency.

Words introduced in the media frequently enlarge into meanings far beyond the scope originally intended for them. How many meanings do the words *Mickey Mouse* have today? Which show approval? Which disapproval?

The term *comic strip* originated in newspapers between 1896 and 1907 when funny situations in comic drawings were strung together in one strip. The two to survive longest were Rudolph Dirks's *Katzenjammer Kids*, which first appeared in 1897, and Richard Outcault's *Buster Brown*, which first appeared in 1902. From these beginnings, we continue to call a section of the newspaper in which the majority of the stories are not the least bit amusing *the comics*. Once a tradition becomes established, it is very hard to change. You can probably list a dozen or more words now accepted in our general vocabulary that originated as part of a slogan, a word of identification in showing approval or disapproval in an entertainment series, or part of an advertising campaign. But more important, really, is the strength of the idea behind the media slogans, the entertainment series, and the advertising.

The impact of the mass media is very strong. It changes our language, stimulates our emotions, informs our intellect, influences our ideas, values, and attitudes. When you were young and absorbing uncritically, you could not possibly know that the majority of the material you saw and heard was designed to produce specific responses from you. Some adults, for that matter, either do not know or refuse to admit the following basic fact of media production: *The* MAJORITY *of material is chosen or designed to produce a predetermined response.* Even that part of media output called "entertainment" is chosen to keep you quiet, unquestioning, available, and receptive to commercial messages inserted throughout. This is evident whether the entertainment is a TV drama with commercials every few minutes or a newspaper or magazine article with columns of type wrapped around the advertisements.

The journalism, news, or information-giving portion of media output is selected, edited, produced, placed in time slots or positioned in the newspaper or magazine to reflect and support the owner's policies. These policies are sometimes intricate and interwoven strands, difficult to isolate individually, because ownership is a giant conglomerate made up of intertwining sections of the current commercial-military-governmental complex. However, no reporter, photographer, film or copy editor, script or continuity writer in either print or electronic media has ever needed to be told specifically what the boss's policies are. You pick them up through your pores within a week or two of accepting a job, and you work accordingly.

The owner's policies, therefore, determine the response that the media wish from you even if it's only to keep quiet and accept. Then the material is written, staged, photographed with or without audio, printed and/or broadcast. We—counted in the millions, the mass audience of mass media—are then programmed to buy, vote, contribute, believe, and support other people's interests, interests which may be commercial, political, charitable, philosophical, or educational. Sometimes these interests will coincide with your own; sometimes they won't. Most of the time, the response comes in as programmed; occasionally it doesn't, or there is an additional, unexpected response. Some of the media's output has long lasting value and worth; some is not only cheap, tawdry, and superficial, but physically, emotionally, and intellectually harmful.

Fortunately for the fate of the nation, the bulk of media material and the built-in responses desired are a combination of good and bad. The important thing is to be able to separate the two. This takes not only knowledge of the media's motivating force, how manipulation is planned and stimuli chosen, but also the maturity and the judgment to make thoughtful decisions.

Great clamorous discussions have been raised through the years about the media as entertainment, the media as art or Art, the media as education, the media as public service, the media as this or the media as that. The media are *all* of these, but any discussion is pointless that does not recognize first the media as money-making businesses, in business to survive and show profit. The development of each medium, historically, follows roughly the same pattern as the development of every big business in the country from steel to breakfast cereal, from automobiles to super-markets. Because industrial, military, and technological growth has erected very large, intricate structures upon this money-making foundation, its basic simplicity has been obscured. Part of this obscurity has been created by natural growth, part by deliberate design. However, once you scrape away the brambles and ivy, pull down the man-made disguises around the foundation, and understand its motivating power, you will be able to judge the realities of the media.

Newspapers, magazines, and other sections of the print medium did not start as a monopoly, but the electronic medium did. Today, however, all media are monopolistic, each segment part of a conglomerate. Television began as a two-network, one-owner monopoly designed to extend and increase radio broadcasting's ability to make money through advertising. Entertainment, information, art, education, public service have always been used as enhancers of all the media's money-making abilities. This is the reality of a commercial society such as ours, and avoidance of this reality avoids consideration of the immediate and the relevant in life today.

Short of convincing all the media to self-destruct on next Fourth of July, there seems no way to redesign them according to a nobler, more altruistic, or ideal pattern. The alternative, therefore, and the main thrust of this text, is to disperse the fog of confusion about the media, created both by time and deliberate effort, so that you can see your options clearly. By the application of scientific methods of collecting data to reach conclusions, you can decide whether to respond or not, literally either to take 'em or leave 'em.

This text, therefore, will be light on history, heavy on today, using *then* primarily as a guide to *now*. It will continually ask you to raise your eyes from this book to look at current media offerings. The guidance offered will be thoughtful questions to ask about the data you collect from current media productions. We will concentrate on *mass* media, pointing out *special audience* media as they influence mass media.

Let us begin by looking around our environment, scientifically checking out the prevalence of the various media, and making a preliminary estimate of their over-all influence in your life.

Activities

1   Media Inventory

   A.   List all the media you observe in an hour or two in the following places:

   (1) In the community in general—in the shopping center or down-town area that you use the most, in the supermarket or grocery store, in the drugstore, at the filling station, at the restaurant or drive-in where you stop for meals or snacks, in any clothing or department store you happen to visit. Include signs, billboards, posters, magazines, displays, radios, TVs, and public address systems.

   (2) At school—in your homeroom, in other classrooms, in general areas such as the cafeteria and hallways. Don't include the library. We all know how loaded it is.

   (3) At home—in your bedroom, living room, dining room or area, kitchen, and bathroom; in the family car or cars, in your car and/or your best friend's.

   B.   Bring your information to class; sort the material into groups of two to four consecutive hours each, and compile your information. Write a list of categories, such as TVs, radios, tape decks, newspapers, magazines, signs, posters, displays—whatever you discovered—down the left side of a sheet of paper and record the number of each, regardless of where you noticed it. The most convenient way to do this is to read down your inventory, item by item, making vertical lines in appropriate categories, with a crosshatch for each five, like this: ||||| ||.

   When you have completed the whole inventory, add the number in each category; then add them all for a grand total of the media in your life.

Discussion

   While you were compiling your inventory, answers to the following questions no doubt presented themselves. You might have mentioned your reactions to your friends and family. Now is a good time to share them with the whole class.

(1) Was it difficult to remember to notice each medium?

(2) Did you find more than you anticipated?

(3) Where did you find the most?

(4) Which medium predominates in your inventory—print or electronic?

(5) What general conclusions did you reach about media?

2   *Media Message Log*

    A.   Now that you know what and how many media your environment contains, let's identify the number and types of responses that you are asked for during a given space of time.

    Choose a two to four hour period from noon to midnight. Divide a piece of paper into two columns. Head one MESSAGE; the other, RESPONSE. As you go through your time period, number and record each message that reaches you and identify the response that it requests. Some requests will be obvious; some, subtle. To get the specifics, ask yourself, "What am I supposed to do?"

    Here are a few examples of what could take place. Pretend this is your last class today. On the way out of the building, a loud-speaker truck drives by, broadcasting for a candidate for mayor. As you reach the street intersection, a red light halts traffic. The radio in the car nearest you is playing. The music stops; you hear a commercial for a used car lot. You take a moment to look at the school newspaper that was distributed earlier. You start an interesting news item on the front page and have to turn to page four to finish it. As you reach the bottom of the column, your eye picks up an ad for shoes. A charitable organization is conducting a fund drive and, on the other side of the street, a man slips a brochure into your hand. You glance at it.

    Here is how you might log these examples:

Message	*Response*
1. Political announcement from truck for candidate for mayor.	Believe information about the candidate. Vote for him or her.
2. Radio commercial for used car lot.	Believe promises of bargains and credit. Buy car.
3. Newspaper ad for shoes.	Believe qualities attributed to shoes. Buy shoes.
4. Brochure telling how ZYX, Inc., helps humanity.	Believe that ZYX, Inc., helps humanity. Give money or time or both.

    Any message that reaches you accidentally is as valid a request for a response as the TV commercials that you know you are going to see when you deliberately choose to watch a sponsored program.

B. Bring your information to class; sort the material into small groups of consecutive hours; analyze your information to answer the following questions. (One group of questions can be used as a discussion guide and the other as an essay guide.)

How many different actions were you requested to take?

If you took these actions, would you benefit? If so, how? If not, who would? How?

If you made a sincere, conscientious effort to perform all the responses requested, how much time, effort, and money would you have to expend?

In the process of receiving these messages, although you were not asked to record it, do you remember receiving any information? Entertainment? What can you now estimate was the approximate proportion of information and entertainment in the messages?

3 Written Assignment

Respond to the following situation either in a short story using dialogue and description or in essay form:

Without using any escape device like running away to a deserted island or camping in the middle of the Mojave Desert, describe how, within the context of your normal life, you could or could not screen or seal yourself from all media messages.

4 Multi-media Assignment

Develop a presentation using still and moving pictures, taped interviews, signs, or placards in which a person attempts to respond to *every* media message that reaches him or her during a given period of time, such as one afternoon. The tone can be either serious or satirical.

*Most people are not particularly critical of mass media
content. . . . Exposure to the mass media gets to be
a deeply ingrained habit. . . . The grip of this habit may
first become visible through personal irritations that
arise with a burned-out television set, a substituted
program, a newspaper strike, or with the failure of a
delivery boy to put the paper on the porch. In moments
like these we become aware of our addiction.*

Otto N. Larsen
Violence and the Mass Media

. . . A long habit of not thinking a thing wrong,
gives it a superficial appearance of being right. . . .

Thomas Paine
Common Sense. January 1776

Chapter 2
Influences of Mass Media

Advance Preparation

1. If the following films or others of similar content are available,
schedule them for showing during discussions of the material in this chapter:

(a) *Federal Government Series: Federal Communications Commission*

(b) Network documentaries of important, controversial subjects that
are now available for use in schools. One such is CBS-TV's program, *Selling
of the Pentagon.*

2. Either by volunteer choice or assignment, look into the *Reader's
Guide to Periodical Literature, The Newspaper Index,* and *The New York
Times Index* for information on the following subjects:

(a) Radio and television station license challenges.

(b) Problems facing the Public Broadcasting System in its relations
with Congress.

(c) Commentary about the initial reactions to the first airing of
Selling of the Pentagon.

10

3. Write Accuracy in Media, Inc., 501 Thirteenth Street N.W., Suite 1012, Washington, D.C. 20004, on school letterhead for their packet of media critiques, especially the one on *Selling of the Pentagon*.

4. Write Television Information Office, 745 Fifth Avenue, New York, N.Y. 10022, on school letterhead and request a room set of the latest booklet reporting results of the survey of *Public Attitudes Toward Television and Other Mass Media*.

5. Write the National Association of Broadcasters, 1771 N. Street, N.W., Washington, D.C. 20036, on school letterhead and request room sets of both the Radio and Television Codes.

6. Write A. C. Nielsen Co., 2101 Howard Street, Chicago, Illinois, 60645, on school letterhead and request a room set of their latest booklet describing Media Research Division services.

7. Invite a representative of a local television station to explain how the Nielsen ratings operate and their effect on programming on his/her station.

Introduction

After you finished the exercises and discussions in Chapter 1, you may have become more aware than ever before of two things: (1) the pervasiveness of mass media in your life, and (2) your frequent lack of personal choice in selecting the messages that request your response. Occasionally the latter situation may be to your advantage. You might otherwise have missed an important event or an opportunity to witness an outstanding performance, purchase a useful item, or mentally grasp a valuable piece of information. As you discovered, however, the bulk of all the messages beamed at you are for another's benefit. The observations you were asked to tabulate were organized to sharpen your awareness of how much is "comin' at you."

The next step is to examine the influence of the mass media and how it is achieved. As you read the following comments, note how they seesaw:

Television and all who participate in it are jointly accountable to the American public for respect for the special needs of children, for community responsibility, for the advancement of education and culture, for the acceptability of the program materials chosen, for decency and decorum in production, and for propriety in advertising. This responsibility . . . can be discharged only through the highest standards of respect for the American home. . . .

Preamble of the Television Code of the
National Association of Broadcasters

. . . Films, television plays, newspaper accounts or magazine stories that stress physical violence, brutality, sexual gratification,
earthy humor, slapstick, or simple melodrama appeal most to
those whose educational backgrounds are limited. . . . In the affluent American society, it is this type of audience member who
. . . has purchasing power in sufficient abundance so that his combined influence on the market can be overwhelming. . . .

> Melvin L. De Fleur
> *Theories of Mass Communication*

. . . An FCC sampling of stations in 1963 found that 40 per cent
had advertising exceeding the code limits. . . . Since the industry
had defined its standards in its own codes and constantly spoke
of them with respect and admiration, it seemed to [FCC Chairman E. William] Henry logical that the FCC should adopt those
standards officially. At license renewal time [every three years]
the FCC could then inquire: has the station observed the industry's own proclaimed standards?

The industry reaction to this was one of horror and outrage;
it stimulated instant countermoves in Congress, where Representative Walter E. Rogers of Texas introduced a bill forbidding
the FCC to take any action to limit commercials. . . . The bill
passed, 317 to 43.

> Eric Barnouw
> *The Image Empire*

Forty-three per cent of the children in the Chicago area had TV
sets at home when we started our surveys in 1949–1950. The
percentages rose rapidly until by 1959, 99 per cent had TV. In
1965, almost all children had access to TV at home, and 36 per
cent in Evanston and Skokie reported having two or more sets.
And many children said that they had color TV.

> Dr. Paul Witty, Northwestern University
> "Studies in the Mass Media—1949–1965"

Robert Sarnoff, in a speech while he was still chairman of corporate NBC, once ventured a definition. He said the public interest
was what the public was interested in. It was patently a definition
to justify broadcasting's excesses in commercial entertainment.
A young child may be *interested* in lighting matches and an
older one in experimenting with drugs, but any parent knows that
neither is in their best interest.

> Les Brown
> *Television: The Business Behind the Box*

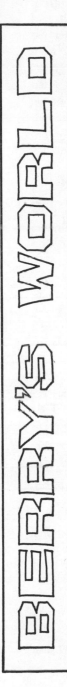

The 40 per cent mortality rate for new programs in any given season means . . . quite simply that the combined appetites of television, the theatre, the moving pictures and even to some extent the print media, are so great that there does not exist sufficient talent to fill all the hours on television and moving picture screens and all the stages that ring Times Square. . . . It often seems to me remarkable that so many good things are done on television . . . and there is no doubt that all media would be better served if there were more such talents available.

> Roy Danish, Director,
> Television Information Office
> *The Shaping of the Television Medium*

. . . the following statistics [were] taken from a recent poll of [members of the Writers Guild of America, West]. Of all who responded:

Eighty-six (86) percent have found, from *personal* experience, that censorship exists in television. Many state, further, that they have never written a script, no matter how innocent, that has not been censored.

Eighty-one (81) percent believe that television is presenting a distorted picture of what is happening in this country today— politically, economically and racially.

Only eight (8) percent believe that current television programming is "in the public interest, convenience and necessity," as required by The Federal Communications Act of 1934, Title 47, U.S. Code, Secs. 307a, 307d.

> David W. Rintels, Chairman,
> Committee on Censorship
> Writers Guild of America, West
> Statement before Senate Subcommittee on
> Constitutional Rights

. . . our present world has moved from gradualness and continuity to a world . . . of Happenings. The world of the Happening is an electronic world of all-at-onceness in which things hit into each other but in which there are no connections. . . . I have found sometimes that it helps to say "the medium is the massage" because the medium is a complex set of events that roughly handles and works over entire populations.

> Marshall McLuhan

As you can see from these opposing viewpoints, not only are the influences of the mass media powerful, but reactions to those influences are equally powerful. Except for De Fleur's and McLuhan's comments, which deal with all media, these comments concern one medium, the most recent one—television. "Had we but world enough, and time," as the poet said in another context, we could document the same kinds of reactions to the other media, starting with books of popular fiction in the 1700s. For a century thereafter, the Establishment felt so threatened by a public that could read that monumental threats, name-calling, and denunciation accompanied each step in the growth of literacy among the general population.

When reading was finally accepted, commercial circulating libraries developed to supply the readers and "guide" them by influencing their thoughts and controlling their expenditures for reading material. Then in the mid-1800s, a new danger appeared—the public libraries. The public, particularly young women and their parents, were warned against the "pernicious and immoral" influences turned loose in the land when this dangerous institution was established. The interlocking monopoly of printer, distributor, and carrier (primarily the railroad) was seriously threatened by public libraries and reacted accordingly. The monopoly would lose control of both publisher and public. By financial and political pressure, politicians, ministers, and other public figures were stimulated to denounce these "houses of sin and degradation."

In the early decades of the 1900s, the type of popular fiction we now beg you to read, if only you'll just *read*, was strongly denounced by parents, teachers, and religious leaders. In the 1930s, analytical writers called commercial radio programming all the dirty names now being used about television, while the broadcast industry said that their programs were varied, educational, and cultural, as it is now claiming for television. Both charges were backed by detailed documentation, as they are today.

In the 1800s, one set of commercial publishers triumphed over another in book distribution. In the 1900s, commercial broadcasting triumphed over educational broadcasting when almost 200 college and university-owned radio stations were driven off the air within a few years. Over thirty years of up-hill and discouraging work went into creating a public educational broadcasting system, and its existence is very shaky because it depends on political influence.

At present, studies of reading habits show that reading has increased as result of watching dramatizations on television, but that it is still meager in comparison with televiewing. Studies also show that vocabularies have increased, particularly in science, and that teachers are more and more suggesting activities connected with televiewing in science, foreign languages, current events, and drama. In addition, courses such as this one have been made part of regular school curricula.

Although the quality of the programs of National Educational Television is increasingly mentioned as influencing young people, their number and availability are miniscule compared to the number and availability of commercial programs. The same comment holds true for thoughtful, serious books and magazines in comparison to superficial publications.

The bulk of the statements of approval seems to come from those connected with promoting television and other media or those whose studies are supported, in part or in full, by some branch of the media. One of the latter is the periodic survey of *Public Attitudes Toward Television and Other Mass Media*, conducted since 1959 by the Roper Organization and paid for by the Television Information Office, the public relations branch of the broadcast industry.

Although the surveys are conducted honorably and useful information about attitudes is collected, need you be told which medium gets the most approval? The assumptions upon which the survey questions are constructed tend to support the status quo. The major general assumption underlying the whole survey seems to capitalize on the fact that change is very frightening to most people. And the threat of change seems to permeate the questionnaires, although, through the years, they have become increasingly complex.

In the interest of attempting to balance the influences of the mass media, the materials from Accuracy in Media, Inc., are an ounce on the other side. Without financial backing from any of the media, print or electronic, AIM has a difficult time reaching the public, but the organization is growing.

Discussion

(1) After the people who collected information about license challenges present their data, consider the following questions: How great is the danger of license challenge to the broadcast industry? Is periodic review of each station's operation a healthful or harmful thing?

(2) Compare the reprints of two sections of the *Congressional Record* in the Appendix. The one dated February 16, 1972, was distributed by AIM; the one dated June 15, 1972, by TIO. Relate the information they contain to contemporary commentary in the print medium, as well as to the content of *The Selling of the Pentagon* film itself. In addition to the discussion that such disparity of opinion will create, consider the following: Two ideas seem to have been overlooked in all the uproar: (1) The film criticizes a government agency for using on the public the same kind of manipulative techniques that every commercial organization, including mass media, uses as its right. (2) The film producers used the same propaganda techniques to make their statement that they claim to be against. Disregarding for a moment your position for or against the military, what are your thoughts about who has the "right" to use such persuasion and propaganda techniques?

(3) After a report about the problems facing the Public Broadcasting

System in its relations with Congress, consider the material presented on the PBS channel in your area. What do you think is the future for PBS? What do you see as its role in your life now and in the future?

Violence in the Media

Two major public concerns about the electronic media are over-commercialization and the exploitation of violence. Commercials will be treated in depth in Chapter 3, *The Impact of Advertising*, but of the two, the exploitation of violence, or "action" and "action-adventure" as it is called within the industry, has elicited the greatest public outcry. Numerous attempts have been made to cut down or eliminate murders, torture, robberies, bombings, kidnappings, lynchings, massacres, and similar horrors from entertainment. So much has been spoken, written, and filmed about the effects of exposure to violence in movies, television, comic books, and magazines that keeping up with it is virtually a career in itself. Charges and countercharges, accusations and denials, studies and re-studies have poured off the presses and out of loudspeakers in such quantity that even a willing mind reels under the assault about nonassault.

Studies concerning the effects of violence on behavior have been financed by citizen committees, colleges and universities, private research organizations, the broadcast industry, and the federal government. Doctors, lawyers, and merchant chiefs have all gotten into the act, with casts of thousands including distinguished members of state and national governments, psychiatrists, psychologists, sociologists, economists, teachers representing the whole spectrum of education from kindergarten to graduate school, and media representatives. A script of events following release of a study usually looks something like this:

Act I: U.S. Surgeon General releases report of his Advisory Committee on Television and Children's Violence entitled *Television and Growing Up: The Impact of Televised Violence*.

Act II: *The New York Times* headlines: "TV Violence Held Unharmful to Youth." Very much smaller paper headlines: "TV Linked to Violence in Young." TIO and industry trade magazines report, "We won! We won!"

Act III: Exposé by two psychologists who worked with the materials before turning them over to the Committee: Psychologists say that the Committee was composed of five network people and seven "independent" scientists approved by the networks, that the published report distorted the data derived from the accumulated materials, and that there is a definite link.

Finale: By whole cast. Song and dance entitled "Here we go again."

The real and long-lasting effect of exposure to violence via the media probably partakes of both viewpoints, intermixed with other influences that create violent and aggressive behavior not yet taken into consideration. A widely quoted statement by Dr. Fredric Wertham, a critic of media violence, said that, when the assassin of President Kennedy, Lee Harvey Oswald, was actually killed on the television screen, some adults didn't believe their eyes; however, "Children blended their realities and knew right off: 'He shot him in the stomach.' This is what always happens in the serials; they had seen it a thousand times."

There are no simple answers to complex questions such as why one person growing up with the media becomes violent while another in the same environment does not. However, growing up with an unrelenting barrage from "an electronic world of all-at-onceness in which things hit into each other, but in which there are no connections," as McLuhan said, *has* to have an influence.

The consistent pattern of cause and effect shown day and night in the media is that problems are solved instantly following an act of violence. Constant repetition of the pattern and consideration of the psychological depths in which attitudes are influenced can lead to such questions as the following:

1. Is it possible that the man who struck the blow that started the 1965 riots in the Watts area of Los Angeles was surprised that, after a short fight, life didn't immediately return to normal?

2. Could people who rioted on one college campus after another in the 60s have expected instant change after their act of violence?

3. What about the subtle influences of media heroes in uniform, firing rifles, in the never-ending wars glorified in the media?

Activities

1. In groups of two, divide the following activities among you: an hour program during prime-time on television, an hour of radio listening, a comic book, and one issue of a newspaper. Total the number of violent episodes found by each group.

2. Have each of the group of two perform one of the following activities, or do them together: Stand before the magazine racks of a large supermarket or discount house and count the number of magazine covers showing scenes of brutality. Do the same at the paperback book racks. Total the number found by each group.

3. Make a grand total of all the episodes of violence and brutality. Based on this specific information, what are your conclusions about the presence of violence in the media?

4. From your survey, discuss the following questions:

(a) Was the violence displayed necessary to get the point across?

(b) What is your reaction to TV programs that show violence and to those that don't? Is there a difference?

(c) What are your feelings about news reports of the real thing? How do you feel when accident victims are shown in the news?

(d) What types of violence other than physical are shown in either print or electronic media?

(e) How does violence in the media compare with violence in real life?

Other Influences of Mass Media

Let's turn our attention now to the subtle, quieter influences of the mass media that have not received as much attention as violence and over-commercialization, but are strong enough to become observable parts of our way of life. These are the attitudes, values, and beliefs that we absorb below the level of active concentration and that are the direct result of growing up with the mass media as part of our accepted, unquestioned environment.

Four major effects observable in behavior patterns among the young include (1) distorted ideas of reality, (2) the 30-minute syndrome, (3) the hot house effect, and (4) the expectation of continuous professional entertainment in all areas of life.

Such effects constitute the main pulse of most mass media offerings, beating away beneath the surface of entertainment, advertising, and information. To explain each and show how they are interwoven, let's use your reactions to your favorite television series as a starting place.

Emotionally, you respond to the acting and the story. You admire the actors, laugh at the jokes, feel fear at the danger, indignation at the injustice, joy at the rescue, satisfaction at the solution, and anticipate the next episode with pleasure.

While experiencing all these emotions, your mind is provided with information, often through background effects. Geographic details, long shots of scenery and cities are usually authentic, even if the rest of the show is filmed in the studio. Although subsidiary to the story's action, some factual information is provided about isolated aspects of medicine, government, law, chemistry, space exploration, teaching, business—whatever the area is that forms the basis of the conflict or problem. This factual information, however limited, is usually accurate, too.

All your reactions so far are on the surface, all easily identified, all easily understood. But on a deeper level of absorption, starting when you were an unquestioning, accepting child, you were not aware of attitudes, philosophies, values, beliefs, and ideas about behavior that you were taking in along with the authentic facts.

Recall the characters in your favorite program. Isn't there a God-like figure who, in the face of universal opposition, successfully solves all problems? The God-like figure is usually male, unless there is a God-like group in which one woman has a role, but she can perform only when surrounded by males. What methods does this male God-like figure or the God-like group use? Ruthless, violent ones? Cooperative, peaceful ones? Which is most approved of, their intellectual or physical ability? If there is any reasoning involved in solving the problem, does the woman contribute? How do these people behave in their self-enclosed world? Your idea of men's and women's roles in the world and your idea of proper behavior have doubtless been influenced by observing God-like figures on television and in the movies or reading about them in popular fiction.

What is the underlying philosophy of your program? That loners are always right, no matter how much being one hurts? That the end justifies the means? That the system is always right or the system is always wrong? That youth is always right and age is always wrong, or the other way around? That a particular solution to a problem will provide happiness forever after? Within each series, the underlying philosophy is the same in every episode, and there it is before you, larger than life, working out successfully time after time after time. Could such massive repetition fail to influence your own attitudes toward life?

According to the writers and producers of these programs, reporting their experiences in 1972 before the Senate Subcommittee on Constitutional Rights, the realities of life in America today are systematically distorted. If you follow one of the medical series, for example, money is never mentioned. No doctor ever charges for his services; no hospital ever bills a patient or denies admittance until a patient can prove his ability to pay the bill. Almost every doctor cures almost every patient, if only the patient will let him. The American Medical Association (which approves the scripts) does not exist and does not act as a pressure group on Congress. Medicare and health insurance also do not exist on the medical programs. Every doctor has endless time to visit with patients, see them off at boats and airports after their cures, attend their parties, and generally act in ways that almost no contemporary physician acts. These are some of the attitudes that form the underlying philosophy of the medical programs. Similarly distorted ones underlie other programs in which some aspect is based on hard fact, such as the operation of police departments, private detectives, and lawyers. Every episode of the program has the same underlying philosophy. Is there any way these distorted attitudes could not become part of your expectations of the real world?

Now look at the cluster of people around the God-like figure. One or two seem quite content to stand forever in his shadow, even though intellectually and physically they are his equal. Have you ever questioned this idea, or did you accept it without thinking as one of the "facts" of life? It is only a fact of this kind of drama, not necessarily a fact of life.

What about male-female relationships? What function does the one woman (why only one?) in this cluster perform? What is her reward at the end of each episode for performing this function? Why does the leading woman in every series about schools *always* teach home economics?

By constant exposure to distortions of reality, people grow up with unreal attitudes, values, and beliefs by which to try to live. Why are such distortions presented? To keep you seated quietly before the television screen, available and receptive to commercials. Or, if you are reading a magazine, available and receptive to the advertisements. All of the mass media are businesses, in business to make money and show a profit.

Your behavior under any circumstance, guided by your attitudes, values, and beliefs, basically reflects a system of right and wrong. It is a personal code of behavior that determines such things as what you are honest about and to what degree and what you call success, prestige, or status—in other words, all those large intangibles that may seem to have no connection with what you do in your spare time, why you chose to join one club rather than another, why you buy a transistor radio or fake a book report, but really are the everyday workings of your personal system of right and wrong.

In addition to personal systems of right and wrong, each country as it grows develops various group philosophies, some of which will overlap yours. These predispositions are utilized by the mass media as hooks upon which to hang entertainment, advertising, and information.

The perfectly ordinary way in which you acquire the major portion of your philosophy of life is by birth. Although a nineteenth century wit once said that the way to be assured of a healthy, wealthy, and otherwise successful life was to choose your grandfather well, no records of people able to do so have ever been discovered. Because you have no control of your ancestry, you have no immediate control over the attitudes, values and beliefs that you inherit as a way of life. Nor can you choose your nationality, color, or creed. Therefore, you start life with quite a large inheritance that you did not choose.

One idea of contemporary psychology is that lack of free choice under every circumstance is bad, bad, bad, not to say terrible. When others are trying to manipulate you for their benefit, clear analytical choice is vital, but who, at age five, is capable of clear analytical choice? How you handle your inheritance, what you keep, what you change, what you throw away are the important aspects of growing up, and the mass media contribute to your choices.

If everyone passively accepted his total inheritance, the transition from one generation to the next would be easy, quiet, and stagnant. The media would have nothing with which to stimulate, excite, shock, thrill, and therefore nothing to sell. They could not sell themselves nor the merchandise which they advertise. But everyone, under local, national, international, and technolgical pressures—all the influences of his own historical time— accepts part, discards part, and changes part of his inherited attitudes, values, and beliefs. As any psychology book will tell you, this behavior is normal, even though it may cause your parents and grandparents to gnash their teeth and utter loud threats, some of which they keep. In their eyes it is as though they gave a boy a complete automobile in good running order and, after driving it around the block, he started making alterations. Or a girl took a brand-new dress, changed the length, threw away the belt, added frills, or, worst of all, returned it for an entirely different style.

Many people consider that the clash of generations has grown sharper, louder, and more disastrous since the end of World War II and during the continuing Korean, Vietnam, and other undeclared wars, with who knows what next to come. Actually, the noise you hear is from the media, and part of the blame for both personal and public disasters belongs to the media. History, in its quiet way, records that social changes were equally great after the Civil War and World War I, although advertising stimulated and hastened them after W.W. I. For example, the generations also fought over long and short hair then, only the other way around. In the 1920s, young people were considered immoral when they cut their hair. In the 1960s, they were considered immoral when they let it grow. Very likely the pendulum will swing back to short hair during the next major social change, unless someone invents a way to grow hair sideways.

The mass media, besides distorting reality, are also quick to take advantage of social change. They habitually seize on current controversies, simplify complex problems, dramatize them, expand on them, sensationalize them, overemphasize them, and sometimes even create them, all as a means of attracting your attention. If it is to their interest, they also tone them down, defuse them, lighten them, restrict them, emasculate them, humor them, or ignore them. These are all aspects of media influence on your behavior at deep levels.

Another way the media make use of your attitudes, values, and beliefs is to play up their conservative aspects, to hold up a mirror in which your beliefs are shown to you in vivid colors, larger than life, and with canned applause that tells you, in effect, that yours are the best of all possbile beliefs, that these are the best of all possible times, and that you are the best of all possible people. Flattering, isn't it? And who can resist such overwhelming flattery, particularly when it is delivered in beautiful packages in the electronic media, both slickly photographed and cleverly acted, and in easy, dramatized reading in the print media, where the differences between fiction and nonfiction are carefully blurred.

The third way the media utilizes your way of life is to seize on both the controversies and the firmly held beliefs, wrap them up in fantasy, and make all your dreams come true. Remember the God-like figure discussed earlier? Wouldn't we all like to be God-like figures? To solve all our own and everyone else's problems easily and then live happily ever after? The mass media do it all for you. Just turn on the fantasy by going to the movies, buying a paperback or magazine, turning on the radio or TV set, and then relax and float away.

Please do not think it wrong or harmful to float away from reality every now and again. We all need to do so. The harmful part is not to know what you are doing. You can then very easily become a victim of manipulation for other's benefit.

These, then, are the three major ways the mass media influence your behavior, as well as capture your attention so that you are available and receptive to response-producing messages:

1. Distorting reality by simplifying, enlarging, or ignoring controversies of current social change.

2. Playing up conservative attitudes, values, and beliefs in a highly flattering manner.

3. Providing a fantasy world in which all your dreams come true.

Discussion

Discuss examples and experiences that either prove or disprove the foregoing analysis of media influence.

The 30-Minute Syndrome

The foundation of the 30-minute syndrome is the idea that major complex problems—personal, national, or international—can be solved simply, that one solution exists for every complex problem, and that profound psychological change can be made easily in one try.

Think back on all the thirty- to sixty-minute stories you have seen on television—they run a little longer in films and novels—and estimate how long *the* solution to *the* problem took. The last three to five minutes on TV? Maybe twelve to fifteen minutes in full-length films? The last chapter in a current novel? A chase, a fight, a few words of explanation, and our Hero, the God-like figure, does it again. Or, for psychological problems of great magnitude, one significant "come-to-realize" conversation acts just like snapping on an electric switch. The troubled person instantly sees the light. *The* problem—as though there were just one—is solved and, immediately, without visible effort, people change forever. No complexities, no difficulties, no backsliding, no time to painfully retrain emotional habits in media-land.

The worst cumulative effect of the 30-minute syndrome is its reinforcement of the idea of instant success. A theoretical equation could be set up as follows: One problem + one try = instant success. Of course, what the media ignore to work out this equation are the facts that the problem is several complex ones intertwined, that one try seldom solves anything, and that there is no such thing as instant success. Even people achieving so-called "over-night success" not only have talent to begin with but usually have long histories of training or practice and have put out great effort.

The effect of watching dramas worked out according to this equation since you were old enough to sit up munching your thumb before the TV set usually reveals itself in two reactions that all teachers can identify. One is a very short span of attention—like thirty minutes. For some students, it is even less. The second is the reverse of instant success. One complex assignment + one try = instant discouragement. Students who are taken in by the media never come to realize that success takes effort, disappointment on occasion, and time, time, time.

The 30-minute syndrome becomes tragedy when young people growing up with the media unknowingly incorporate these superficial ideas into their emotional depths and try to live according to them. Such children will never be successful because emotional problems, even normal growing-up problems, are not subject to rapid change, nor are solutions to complex problems ever simple and simply achieved.

The Hot House Effect

The "hot house effect" means, quite simply, pushing young people into maturity earlier than their emotional development can handle it. The quickened pace of life in this country since the end of World War II, both mirrored and stimulated by all the media, seems to require ten-year-olds to act like fifteen-year-olds, fifteen-year-olds to act like twenty-year-olds, and twenty-year-olds to act with the wisdom that requires another ten to fifteen years to develop.

Emotions are not electricity. They do not develop in microseconds. Having a piece of information at age fifteen does not equal having the maturity to use it wisely. Learning the difference between thinking and emoting is a major way to control the "hot house effect" so that it does not control you. Acquiring this control will give you a true freedom of choice.

The "hot house effect" has resulted in a nationwide youth orientation. No one knows exactly where this phenomenon started, but it is now part of the American way of life to rush youngsters forward to twenty and oldsters backward to twenty-nine and a half, ages at which everybody freezes for eternity. People your age trying to act too old and adults trying to act too young make life difficult for everyone. The hot house effect seems to stimulate people, both young and old, to do things that, prior to the subtle influence of the mass media, they would never have done, or at least, not so fast nor so sweepingly.

Professional Entertainment in Your Life

As more and more easily available professional entertainment pours into your life, the latest being video casettes, your ability to recognize high standards of performance increases. Your level of sophistication about what makes a "good" show gets higher each year until, by the time you reach high school, you not only expect to be entertained all the time, but expect it at a professional level. Religious leaders, parents, and teachers who are not natural comics, who have not practiced routines, who cannot reel off a string of gags, who cannot ad lib amusing repartee, who can not sing and dance, are at a disadvantage.

Sesame Street, The Electric Company, and similar programs for pre-schoolers do a wonderful job of preparing children for school, with one unfortunate side effect. The nation is applauding the success of entertainment that teaches. With what expectations do six-year olds with a year or two of Sesame Street behind them face their first-grade teachers? With what expectations for entertainment do you enter your classes? It's something to think about.

Conclusions

Some people say that putting the electronic medium completely out of business or controlling all the media would solve our problems. Some people have placed the blame for race riots, student militancy and other disastrous disruptions on media stimulation and irresponsible sensationalizing to attract attention. Part of these accusations are probably true, but shutting off or controlling the media (by whom? to what extent?) seems akin to the idea that cancer will go away if we do not talk about it.

Others claim that the materialistic orientation of society is due to the soft-sell, hard-sell and in-between-sell that reaches you from the media all day, every day. Without this commercial emphasis, love, brotherhood, altruism, and similar good things would be more in control of the world. No doubt part of this is true, too, but history has records of communities that started as experiments in love and brotherhood, but failed within a short time because of what appears to be man's basic urge to compete and collect possessions. Civilization from its start has been commercial, and commerce itself is not bad. But the way people handle it can be bad and frequently is. As long as people are going to compete, they themselves must control how it is to be done.

In reaction to the print media, you can write letters to the editor or author of a work you object to or wish to question. In reaction to the electronic media, you can write letters to the broadcasting system, the program producer, or the advertiser, but generally most people do not exert themselves. Even if you do, it is *after* the event. Response, even protest, *after* the event is the media's biggest advantage. From the media to you is a one-way street, and the number of responses to the messages sent down that one-way street, packaged in a fantasy of information and entertainment, is their measure of success. Each medium is a business, in competition with all the others for your attention, your money, your vote, your belief. Each year the pace increases, and the media people have to find new ways to attract your increasing sophistication and ever shorter span of attention. Otherwise they would go out of business.

In the same way that commerce itself is not bad, the media themselves are not basically at fault. The fault lies in the way they are being used. Both the public and the media owners must take responsibility for bringing about change. You on your part can learn to detect manipulative devices, misleading, and unfair emotional appeals, then give such techniques the weight they deserve in forming opinions, making decisions, casting votes, and spending money. If necessary, you can stop watching, listening, and buying, a reaction that will cause the media owners and advertisers to change their presentations more quickly than any other.

Activities

1   Conflicts About Social Change
    A.   *Class Discussion*—Consider the current national controversies about behavior changes that people your age are involved in: Race relations; the changing roles of women in politics, business, and the professions; the changing roles of men inside the home and with children; premarital sex, availability of abortion, and rise of venereal disease among youth; results of the legal change of the age of maturity to eighteen; drug use and abuse; and changes in attitudes toward attending college, to name just a few issues.

    Choose one controversy important to you, and then investigate how it is being handled in the media. Decide whether or not the media treatment falls into the simplify-and-solve category or the defuse-or-ignore category.

B. *Individual reports*—Use one of the following guidelines in either a written or oral composition, multi-media, or motion picture report:

(1) If the controversy in part A falls into the simplify-and-solve category, how is it being handled? What aspects are left out?

(2) If the controversy falls into the defuse-or-ignore category, present ways in which you think it could be handled positively in the media.

2 Age Survey

Make an age survey of people you see or hear in both print and electronic media. For example, using one issue of a national magazine, estimate the age of each person pictured or written about. Do the same for several hours of radio listening and several of televiewing. Include ads in print and commercials on the air. Discuss the results in class.

3 Media Presentations

Media people defend themselves from accusations that their facilities are being abused by pointing to the numbers of people watching television, listening to radio, attending movies, reading magazines and newspapers, and saying, "This is what the people want." Critics reply by stating, "What you get becomes so customary and so familiar that it becomes what you want. People really have no choice." Discuss the merits of both comments.

4 Information Survey

A. During your regular media use, make a list of *new* subjects that you learn about. In the electronic media, take into account the background material of all series episodes, movies, and anything dramatized, as well as the subjects of specials and documentaries. Use all contents of print media.

Choose three subjects that stir your curiosity. Remember, these should be new subjects, not the same old things you've used in reports before. After a conference with your teacher, settle on one to investigate further. Stay away from encyclopedias and books. Use newspapers, news magazines, popular magazines, special audience magazines, and any radio or tape material that is appropriate.

In your report, either oral, written, film, or multi-media, identify as nearly as you can what information came from which source, as well as what information was repeated in all sources. The purpose of this assignment is not only "to scratch an itch" (that is, to satisfy your curiosity), but to discover what kind of information comes from where.

B.   Either in your school or public library, find a magazine published specifically for your age group and sex before World War II. Choose one issue. Then find a current issue of a magazine published specifically for your age group and sex, either one that you read regularly, one from a newsstand, or one from a library if the library allows current issues to circulate.

Compare the fiction in the two from the standpoint of what behavior was considered permissible in the 1930s and what behavior is permissible now. What language was used then compared to the language used now? What attitudes were expressed about "good" and "bad" then and about "good" and "bad" now?

Compare the nonfiction from the standpoint of what subjects were considered acceptable for people your age in the 1930s and what subjects are considered acceptable today. What are the differences in general presentation?

The results of this comparison may be reported orally or in writing.

C.   Borrow from the public library one book in any of the following series: Horatio Alger, Tom Swift, the Rover Boys, Nancy Drew or any other popular series of two or more generations ago. These series, incidentally, were very popular with young people and very unpopular with their parents. Many a Tom Swift was read under the bedclothes by flashlight. Many a Nancy Drew was camouflaged by something more "uplifting." Compare the ideals of behavior then with the ideals of behavior today.

*If television can be said to have any values at
all, it is those of the salesmen, big businessmen,
manufacturers, and showmen who control it. . . .*

Harry J. Skornia
Television and Society

*. . . a consumer who is persuaded by an advertisement
is also yielding to his desire or willingness to be counted
in a group—a community of consumers. . . . The
democracy of cash is probably one of the most
real and present and unadulterated democracies in
history. . . . From the moment of our rising in the
morning, the breakfast food we eat, the coffee we drink,
the automobile we drive to work—all these and nearly
everything we consume becomes a thin, but not
negligible, bond with thousands of other Americans.*

Daniel J. Boorstin
"Welcome to the Consumption Community"

Chapter 3
The Impact of Advertising

Advance Preparation

1. Call the nearest television station and ask the Station Manager or
Advertising Manager to save films of commercials marked "Discard After
Use" by the advertising agency. The biggest agencies, handling the accounts
spending the most advertising money, usually do this as the cheapest and
easiest way of handling the thousands of "dupes" they distribute for use
during a "station break." The duplicate commercials are 16mm films which
can be shown through standard movie projectors. A student photographer
or technician in the Audio-Visual Aids Department can splice all those
pertaining to the same product for use later in this chapter. (Note: Some
advertising agencies are beginning to use video tape rather than film
because of the higher quality of reproduction. However, this practice

29

is not yet widespread because of cost. If your school owns video tape equipment, you might borrow some of these commercials; however, you won't
be able to splice and group the material, and the tapes could accidentally
be erased.)

2. Bring in a collection of full-page, full-color magazine and newspaper advertisements of major brand products and representative institutional ads of companies or organizations selling services. The products
chosen might include, for example, automobiles, food, beverages, cosmetics,
clothing, furniture, soaps, deodorants, and major and minor electrical appliances. As institutional ads, collect those sponsored by banks, insurance
companies, income tax preparation offices, utilities such as gas, electricity,
and telephone, and organizations supported by public contribution. All
these ads will be used later in the chapter.

3. Tape record the commercials only, one after another, from an hour
of radio time for use later in this chapter.

4. Telephone the local District Attorney's office to arrange a visit
from a lawyer who handles fraudulent advertising cases to discuss laws
and legal procedures available to citizens.

5. If a Federal Trade Commission Field Office is reasonably close,
arrange a visit from a representative to explain the FTC's functions,
strengths, and limitations.

6. Invite a representative of the local Better Business Bureau to
describe the operation of this organization.

It might be valuable to arrange a panel discussion of representatives from these offices, followed by a question-and-answer period. Whether
their appearances are individual or collective, each member of the class
should prepare questions in advance, following study of the relevant section of this chapter.

Introduction

As result of completing the activities in the first two chapters, you
now have a clearer idea not only of the pervasive influence of the mass
media on your life, but also of some of the ways this influence is brought
to bear. As you discovered in your studies of entertainment, the strongest
influences are those that subtly penetrate your attitudes, values, and beliefs while you're actively engrossed in plot and people. Now let's consider
another influential and pervasive media element: advertising.

Advertising comprises the largest and least subtle part of all the material that has been designed to produce predetermined responses. In *prod-*

uct advertising, you are supposed to respond by buying a specific brand product. In *institutional* advertising, you are supposed to respond by recalling and admiring whatever "good guy" image the manufacturer or service corporation has been trying to create. If this organization should, just by accident, you understand, also sell products, well, you know the next step—you are to relate the "good guy" image to the quality of the product.

Advertising also uses the three major ways that the media use to capture and hold your attention. It (1) distorts reality by simplifying, magnifying, or ignoring the controversies of current social change; (2) flatteringly reflects conservative attitudes, values, and beliefs; and (3) provides fantasy worlds in which all dreams not only come true, but do so instantly. In advertising you need not wait even thirty minutes for success, fame, fortune, or a simple solution to complex problems. In the print media, one quick glance at an advertisement achieves it all. An electronic commercial requires only thirty seconds for instant persuasion, instant beauty, instant promotion, instant success, instant cure, instant solutions to take place.

The "community of consumers," which historian Daniel J. Boorstin, quoted on the first page of this chapter, has called us, came into existence as a result of two industrial movements that started in the same era. One was the mass production of thousands of items of clothing and equipment needed by the Civil War armies, and the conversion of the means of production to civilian manufacturing after the war ended. The other was a retailing revolution that changed selling from a person-to-person or small-merchant-to-individual-customer transaction to the impersonal one of large department stores and mail order houses.

Even though a single person such as John Wanamaker in Philadelphia, R. H. Macy in New York, Marshall Field in Chicago, and Morton D. May in Los Angeles, started his own "merchandising palace," most large department stores are now only a part of the diversified holdings of giant corporations.

With the ability to appeal to masses of people by offering mass-produced personal and household items, business and sports equipment, and the like, each item indistinguishable from all the others of the same kind, advertising became the force that not only welded together, but also expanded, the consumer community. Advertising created "the more you consume, the better person you are" mystique, and has almost made "Join the fun! Buy now!" the national philosophy.

In the following chapter, you will discover the working relationship between advertising and the media and how advertising uses your captured attention to produce predetermined responses.

Activities—Space and Time Allocation Studies

1 Electronic Media

    A.   Either by volunteer choice or assignment, have each student watch an hour of television and listen to an hour of radio, making sure that all times of day and types of programs are covered for all stations in the area. (Note: A newscast is a "program.")

    If your school has classroom radio and television sets available or people can bring in portables, start this study at school. This will provide both a representative hour of daytime programming and verification of procedure. In research projects, the truth and acceptance of conclusions usually depends upon everyone recording observations in the same way.

    Prepare a Time Allocation Chart for each program like the one shown.

Time Allocation Chart

Station Call Letters ———— Radio/TV ———— Network ——— Date ———

Program name ————————— Number of minutes ——— Time ————

Number of commercials during program ————————— Total ————
    (Note: Record a slash mark for each commercial as it starts, then count
            up total at the end of the program.)

Number of commercials during station break ————— Total —————

Figuring thirty seconds per commercial, deduct total number of minutes of commercials from total program time. Remainder —————

    Percentage of time for program   —————
    Percentage of time for advertising —————

    Collate Time Allocation Charts according to day and night time slots. Divide into groups according to time of programming, list kinds of programs broadcast during that time slot, analyze the figures, and then report answers to the following questions in class:

    (1) What do the percentages tell about time allocation during the programs? During station breaks?

    (2) Is there a difference in time allocation among programs broadcast at different times of day and night? Between different kinds of programs?

    (3) What are the differences in time allocations between local and network programs?

2   Print Media

    Bring to class the following issues of the newspapers your family reads: Sunday, Monday, and Saturday for all papers; Wednesday for afternoon papers; and Thursday for morning papers. If you can, collect the same issues of representative small dailies and large metropolitan newspapers. Also include papers published in Spanish, German, Polish, Yiddish, Japanese, or Chinese, and papers published for Black as well as for White readers. Since most people are likely to read the same local papers, the library collection can supplement. After using the papers here, save them for the activities in Chapter 5.

Also bring to class back issues of magazines. Try to have these represent women's, men's, news, and sports magazines, as well as those appealing to special audiences. Aim for a representative ethnic mix. Get November and December, August and September issues for comparison.

Either by volunteer choice or assignment, form into two groups (one for newspapers and one for magazines) and fill out the Space Allocation Chart shown for each issue of each newspaper and magazine. The *date* of the newspaper is not important here; the *day* is. The month is important for magazines.

Space Allocation Chart

Name of paper or magazine ————————— Day or date ————

Total number of pages —————————.

Number of full pages of advertising —————————

Number of full pages of news, articles, stories, photographs, or other information —————————

Number of pages of part advertising and part information or entertainment
—————————

Measure number of inches of advertising per page; add totals; and place grand total here: —————————

Measure number of inches of news, articles, stories, photographs, and other information; add totals; and place grand total here: —————————

    Percentage of advertising   —————————
    Percentage of everything else —————————

When the charts are completed, collate them according to the day for newspaper issues and the month for magazines. Analyze the figures according to the day or the month, and then report your answers to the following questions:

    (1) What do the percentages tell about space allocation in the print media?

    (2) In what way are Monday's and Saturday's papers alike? Sunday's and Wednesday's or Thursday's?

(3) In what way are November and August magazine issues alike? September and December?

(4) What are the major differences in space allocation on different days for newspapers and on different months for magazines?

What Advertising Does

As a result of the empirical evidence tabulated in the foregoing studies, you have discovered that the role played by advertising in the media is more than a large one. At this moment in mass media's history, in fact, they could not survive without advertising. It pays the bills and provides the profits. In itself, advertising is a three to four billion dollar annual business, and growing. The largest advertiser in the country spends about $100 million annually, and many spend an average of $10 million a year. A thirty-second commercial during a prime time television program costs about $70,000, and the cost is still rising.

Advertising, therefore, is the reason your interest is "teased" so that you will remain before the television set until "after the following message" even for the weather report, which, after all, is provided *free* by the government. Advertising is the reason both radio and TV talk shows have available a steady stream of guests, each promoting something, from charitable organizations to new movies. Even books, which are not advertised in the electronic media, get plugged if the author is available for personal appearances. Talk shows, particularly local ones, have always been a press agent's gravy train. You can put guest after guest on these programs with no strain except having to get up early in the morning for A.M. shows or stay up late at night for P.M. shows. Advertising is the reason newspaper and magazine articles are continued to back pages, and why a media personality's ability to create audience loyalty is more important than any other ability.

Without the demands of advertising for advances in technology, possibly some of the developments in art and art materials, photography, use of color, film animation, and other behind-the-scenes production techniques might not have occurred. But also, without advertising, all the linguistic creativity of copy writers might have been applied to other kinds of writing, and some sensitive, talented writers might have been spared the ulcers, nervous breakdowns, broken homes, and messed up children that the destructive pressures of their work help to create.

Without advertising, possibly its leaders' competitive energy and charisma, not to mention their organizational and selling abilities, would have been used in other areas of life. It is even entirely possible that civilization could have advanced without being made overwhelmingly conscious of the psychological damage of odors, for example, or the ability of coffee to save marriages, but we'll never know. We may have to go down in history as the commercial civilization with a very limited vocabulary, for whom "play a game" really meant "buy something," for whom "join the fun" really meant "buy something," for whom "get involved" really meant "buy something," for whom "love thy neighbor" really meant "buy something," for whom "the whole family can do it and it's fun, too" really meant "buy something." If our civilization is judged by advertising only, all experience will be considered a consumer activity.

How Advertising Does It

At this time in your life, you are probably finding that childhood's simplicities are not exactly the whole story. Every aspect of life and your relationship to it is becoming more and more complex. Intellectually, your teachers are requiring that you develop your ability to consider several ideas and attitudes simultaneously. So does advertising, with the added dimension of stimulating your fears and hopes, then asking you to make decisions based on the "logic" of those emotional reactions.

However, before we can deal with the over-all impact of advertising, we must sort its complexity into individual components, identify the effects of each component, and see how each effect contributes to that impact. To achieve this goal, we will limit this chapter to national commercial advertising of major brand products in everyday use by millions of people. These products include automobiles, food, beverages, cosmetics, clothing, non-prescription medications, items of personal grooming, furniture, major and minor electrical appliances including the electronic media themselves—in fact, just about anything you and your family use daily. Lift your eyes from this page. The first thing you see probably has been widely advertised. Yes, even if you are reading this in a school classroom. Everything from the desk you are sitting at to the chalk the instructor uses has been part of a planned and organized advertising campaign. The school items were advertised in "special audience" media; the home items, in the mass media.

The quality of advertising ranges from very good through all the shades and combinations of good and bad to very bad. The advertisers themselves range from individuals who are ethical, humanistic, and responsible in their dealings with the public to those who are criminally fraudulent, greedy, and irresponsible. The highest quality of creativity in art, use of words, and depth of accurate information can be found combined with the lowest kind of manipulative devices in a single advertisement or series of advertisements. (A series is called a "campaign.") This powerful combination delivers its impact all at once, and each of us responds all at once. However, after learning to sort out the various aspects of the impact, we can choose what we will respond to, what we will discard, and then decide whether or not we will buy the product on its merits.

Before we go into the production of advertising for the media, let's first establish our point of departure.

Exactly what *is* advertising? Or does that question seem in the same category as what is a football game? Oh, everybody knows *that*, you would say immediately to the football question, and you would be entirely correct to a point. You could answer the question about advertising correctly, too, to that same point. However, since you are growing up in a culture where you are bombarded by advertising from the day you are born, just reaching that point is not going far enough.

What is a football game? It is a contact sport in which two opposing teams of eleven men each compete for the high score by attempting, in a variety of ways, to carry a ball over a goal line or kick it over a goal post.

What is advertising? It is an arrangement of words or words and pictures in print, with motion and sound added on television, or an arrangement of only words and sounds on radio—all designed to persuade you to buy a product or service.

As general definitions, each of these is correct, but both are severely limited by dealing only with the superficial, easily seen elements of the game and the industry. These are truly what everybody knows, and this is our point of departure. From now on, we will be concerned with the elements of advertising that lie beneath the surface and form the basis upon which the decisions about how to use the surface elements are made.

To identify the elements underlying advertising, let's use the football game analogy once more. Stop reading for a moment, take out a piece of paper and list as many emotions as you can think of connected with football. Start with *fear*, as in fear of losing a game.

Now make a list of as many abstract ideas as you can think of connected with football. If you start with the idea of *status*, as in the status of attending a school with a high-ranking team, you will be in right field. Some items might appear on both lists, depending on your definitions of emotions and ideas. The line between the two sometimes is not very exact.

Read through your two lists and apply the emotions and ideas to advertising. Recall a TV commercial shown in "prime time" (from 6 P.M. to 11 P.M.) for any national brand product in one of the categories listed earlier. The chief emotions, such as fear and hope, and the important abstract ideas, such as status, success, and security, form the foundation upon which that commercial was designed.

Advertisements in the print media combine visual art and printed words in a "layout," a planned arrangement that makes maximum use of every inch of space bought in the newspapers and/or magazines chosen to "run" an ad. Even the use of white space is in the plan to help create the effect decided upon. The advertiser buys time, not space, in the electronic media, starting with ten-second segments, with thirty-second segments the most frequently used. These time segments are called "spots."

In radio commercials, music and sound effects take the place of visual art, rare but occasional moments of silence take the place of white space, and the words are read by actors who can produce the voice sound chosen to create the planned effect. Television commercials combine all the elements of both print and radio advertisements with an added dimension, the camera, which can make this especially planned and organized world come alive for half a moment. Most TV commercials, however crowded with people, sound, and movement, are thirty-second spots. Skilled, creative camera work is one of the most effective methods of delivering the planned impact.

In all print and electronic advertising, the key method of creating a planned effect and maintaining it in the receiver's psychology—not his logical mind, but his illogical emotions—is *repetition*. Repetition of key words, phrases, slogans, sounds and sound effects, appearances, facial expressions and specific movements by the actors and actresses help create and maintain the desired reaction in the reader/listener/viewer who, for thirty seconds, becomes a participant in an imaginary world. The advertiser hopes that repetition of the total impact, particularly if the same campaign is released simultaneously in all the media, will result in your believing so deeply and so strongly in his product that you will buy it in spite of competition from many other products that are essentially the same. The people who produce advertisements that can compel a belief that strong and lasting, called "brand loyalty," are literally worth their weight in gold to the manufacturer.

To discover the psychological impact in a single advertisement/commercial and relate it to a whole campaign that has been going on for some time, even years, you will have to discard an idea that most people have. The idea is that advertising is selling products. That idea may have been true when all advertising consisted of announcements saying that such-and-such a product is available and where. A few ads still do no more than that, but they are in the minority. Action to purchase a specific product or service is, of course, the desired end result, but advertising no longer relies on the virtues of the product itself to stimulate this action. Since the late 1800's, as newspaper and magazines ads show, advertising has been stimulating fear and selling hope.

The fears and hopes played upon by commercial advertising are usually two sides of the same thing. For example, fear of loneliness and hope for popularity, fear of ugliness and hope for beauty, fear of being an old maid and hope for marriage, fear of not having status and hope for status, fear of old age (like thirty-five) and hope for continued youth (remember the "hot house effect"?), fear of insecurity and hope for security, fear of illness and hope for health, fear of family break-up and hope for continued family happiness, fear of having no sex appeal and hope of having a great deal, fear of dullness and hope for excitement.

This list of hopes and fears is only partial because it is impossible to cover all the combinations and anticipate all the inventions of the highly talented people who create advertisements and use events and crises of the moment for springboards. However, you can consider the following when trying to identify any hope-fear combination in current use.

When the country was all stirred up about the idea of having fun, fun, fun, advertising reflected and helped stimulate the idea. When the country was all stirred up about increasing dehumanization, advertising sold love and involvement. When the country was stirred up about pollution, advertising sold ecology. When an energy shortage occupied the news, advertisers sold conservation. When the major oil companies noted increasing reference to their profit-oriented, monopolistic goals, their advertising increased, pointing out their "good guy" attitude and "relentless efforts on the public behalf."

An ad agency speaker recently advised representatives of retail drug stores that their young woman customer had become convinced that drugs are exorbitantly overpriced and that mouthwashes accomplish nothing. "She doesn't believe skin creams can remove wrinkles, but she knows that some detergents can remove skin; therefore, I'll tell her about my cosmetics that meet today's *real* skin needs—protection from the environment. For instance, I'll tell her that if the air has become so polluted it's beginning to corrode statuary, think what it's doing to her skin!" Notice the same old scare tactics based on the same unrelated relationships. What are they scaring people with now? The appliance people, with consumer protection an issue, are now selling consumer protection as the reason to buy the same appliances they sold to make women super-housewives and men super-brilliant check writers. How many advertisers sell family fun, family nutrition, family energy, family love, family this and family that?

Activity—How to Interpret Advertising

1   Print Media

Place before you a full-page color advertisement from the current issue of a popular magazine for one of the major products in the national brand categories listed earlier.

Look at the ad. What is pictured in the background? A country club? An expensive home or a room in one? An elaborate office? A clean, shining, up-to-date garage? An ideal vacation spot or a small section of a magnificently kept wooded area or lakeside? Or what? There *will* be a background, and it was put there to stimulate your hopes and fears. What does it represent? Status? Love? Popularity? Success? Excitement? Youth? Pleasure? Security? Or what? The background of an ad, whether the one in print before you or in the commercials you see on television, is there to help stimulate some fear and to say, symbolically, that buying this particular product will provide the means to overcome that fear, thereby giving you hope.

Now consider the foreground. This may show either the product by itself or with people around it, admiring or using it. If people are admiring or using the product, what kind of people are they? Young? Handsome men and beautiful women? The young married group? Singles? The teenage market? A happy family? If there are children, what kind are they? Any ugly, really messy, misbehaving types? Look at the expressions on their faces. Aren't they a happy, satisfied, successful lot? And you know how they got that way, don't you? Of course, by buying The Product. What you are supposed to do is to "identify with" or imagine yourself to be a part of that idealized picture of success and beauty, to make an emotional leap that attributes all your own hoped-for-success to The Product and then to run right out to buy one. If it's small, buy two. If it's on sale, buy three. In the wonderful world of advertising, you do something known as "saving money" by spending three times the amount you originally intended or actually can afford.

The implied emotional relationship to you, the potential buyer, is probably the original and still the most popular use of art in advertising. You are supposed to identify psychologically with the pictured representations of the ideal, become a participant in the life they are living, and relate that ideal life to the product being peddled.

And right here, before we even look at the words, the analysis becomes murky with complexities. The art you are looking at, as well as the moving art on television commercials, is of the highest quality. Some of the best artists in the country are hired to manipulate your emotions so that you will buy one product rather than another just like it, or any product whether or not you actually need it.

Switch off, for a moment, the emotional connections suggested by the art and look objectively at the techniques represented by this one ad before you now. Does it make use of photography, painting, line drawings, or a combination of these? If it is photographic, can someone in class who is a photographer comment on the technique? Were there any tricks used to produce the picture? Does the food spilled on the carpet not sink in because there is a sheet of glass or a piece of clear plastic to prevent any damage? Comment about other types of art. Are the details exaggerated? Does the automobile, for example, look longer, bigger, shinier than it is when viewed standing on its own four wheels in the street? Are the people out of proportion in size to the product? The exaggerations and tricks are part of both the artistry and emotional manipulation.

Now look at the words, taking the largest line of print first. What kind of word usage appears in that headline? A slogan? A scare? A laugh? Is it a play on words, such as "We're Growing on Your Account," used by a bank; "Be a Knowbody," used by an advice-giving organization; or "We're Minding Everyone's Business," used by a firm of business consultants? It could be an adaptation of a well-known phrase, such as "The Wizard of Ahs" for a restaurant; of a popular saying, such as "Here Today, There Tomorrow," used by a furniture mover; or of a popular song lyric, such as "So Long, Ol' Paint," used by a paint store to advertise a sale. Or is the headline some variation of "NOW . . . AT LAST IT'S HERE . . ." announcement? The purpose of the headline is to attract your attention, lead your eye to the pictures, then down into the body of the copy. The copy may appear under the pictures with or without other, smaller subheadlines.

At first glance, you might think that the use of the words isn't very important, that little attention is paid to them because few people probably do more than glance at the headlines and ignore the small type. Very likely this is truth for the majority of print advertisements. That's one reason why fewer and fewer words per inch are being used. However, on radio and television, where the words are read aloud by actors, they have increased importance.

What was your reaction to the headline? Did it make you feel good? Stir your curiosity? Contribute to the fear-hope stimulation? The words should have; they were written to do one or the other, preferably all three at once. The copy writers, like the artists and photographers, are usually top talent in the advertising world. Their words are supposed to increase the impact of the total advertisement by triggering connotations, which are your emotional reactions to certain words. Your reactions depend on past experiences with the ideas represented by the words. Of course, the copy writers try for favorable connotations to enhance the planned emotional reaction. If some word or two in the early part of the copy triggers unfavorable connotations, the rest of the copy will tell how you can use the product to overcome all the bad reactions.

If the copy goes into technical details about the chemical composition of the product, the mechanics of manufacture, or the "results" of research or surveys supporting the value of the product, very few of these "facts" can be checked out. Specific details are either left out or deliberately obscured. The flow of art and language that produces the fearhope syndrome is supposed to prevent questioning.

What words, phrase, or slogan are repeated? Traditionally, the slogan or most important selling words are repeated four times in a large ad or thirty second commercial. Remember that repetition is the key method of hammering the response-producing message into the potential customer.

Now sit back and consider the advertisement as a whole. How do the components of the emotional impact relate to the merits of the product? Are the promised results something that the product can deliver or that the product has any relationship to? Or are the advertisers asking logical people to believe that a wife's rough hands or a husband's hair dressing might actually cause their marriage to break up? That popularity, excitement, status, sex appeal, and perpetual youth can be achieved by serving one kind of beverage rather than another? Will lack of the product *really* produce the blight upon your life the advertiser is predicting?

Throughout this entire discussion of the manipulative techniques of advertising, a technique was borrowed from advertising itself—the technique of repetition. The idea of planning—the planned response to the planned stimulation created by the planned arrangement—was repeated numerous times to call your attention to the fact that advertising is the product of human designs. People are the planners and producers of advertising, and by working backward from the finished advertisement, we can arrive at the way it was planned, executed, and placed for its moment of life in the media.

2   Electronic Media

A.   Using the films of commercials collected from the television station and grouped according to product, identify the fear-hope combination, slogan, play on words, or "point of sale" phrase that is repeated most often, and then consider the following aspects of TV commercials that influence your reactions:

What do the actors and actresses look like? What effect is their age intended to create?

Describe the announcer's voice. Is it soothing as though preventing the thought of anything unpleasant? Is it confidential as though speaking only to you, with nothing said for public information? Is it irritating? Is it urgent? The announcer's voice quality is part of the planned effect.

What about the music? Is it soft and dreamy? Loud and triumphant? Does it suggest spring, the joys of motherhood, the beauty of romance, the pride of achievement? Or what?

Do the commercials offer examples of instant persuasion, instant success, instant change, instant reconciliation, instant beauty, instant recovery, or a similar miracle?

B.   Run the radio tapes of the radio commercials, using the questions from the TV study that apply. In these commercials, the music and the announcer's voice are vital in creating the fear-hope reaction.

Conclusions

The following questions can be used for class discussion, formal panel discussion, or written, oral, or multimedia essays:

(1) After years of absorbing attitudes, values, and beliefs via the 100,000 commercials every high school graduate is estimated to have seen, what might be thought a woman's primary concern? A man's? Describe this woman's and this man's idea of a successful life.

(2) If a person from another planet were to judge our values entirely by our advertising in both print and electronic media, what would he conclude about the American Way of Life?

(3) Check through the last few years in *Reader's Guide to Periodical Literature* and find an article critical of advertising. Then find an article written for a trade magazine such as *Advertising Age, Printer's Ink, Broadcasting, Television, Television Age,* or *Advertising Agency.* Compare the information, tone, and attitudes.

(4) The following was written in 1963 by Betty Friedan in her book, *The Feminine Mystique:*

> . . . those deceptively simple, clever, outrageous ads and commercials that an observer . . . accepts as fact that the great majority of American women have no ambition other than to be housewives. . . . Their unremitting harangue is hard to escape in this day of mass communications. . . . They have made it part of the fabric of [a woman's] everyday life, taunting her because she is not a better housewife, does not love her family enough, is growing old.

Are these charges still true? Collect several samples of advertising and commercials that you think Ms. Friedan's statement might describe and explain how they prove her point. What are the men's roles in these ads and commercials?

Social Change and Advertising

Well documented economic studies and publication of statements by George Washington Hill of the American Tobacco Company have established the fact that advertising was the greatest force among several in making smoking cigarettes by women socially acceptable, thereby doubling sales. Although men have smoked cigarettes since the 1880s, large annual

"We know our Luckies
That's how we stay slender"

EVERY woman who fears overweight finds keen interest in new-day and common-sense ways to keep a slender, fashionable figure. Overweight must be avoided. "Better to light a Lucky whenever you crave fattening sweets."

Toasting does it. Toasting develops and improves the flavor of the world's finest tobaccos. Lucky Strike satisfies the longing for things that make you fat, without interfering with a normal appetite for healthful foods. That's why Luckies are good to smoke. Toasting makes *Lucky Strike the healthy cigarette for you to smoke.*

Many men who carefully watch their health discovered this years ago. They know that Luckies steady their nerves and do not slow up their physical vigor—prominent athletes have gone on record that this is so. They know that 20,679 physicians have stated that Luckies are less irritating to the throat than other cigarettes.

A reasonable proportion of sugar in the diet is recommended, but the authorities are overwhelming that too many fattening sweets are harmful and that too many such are eaten by the American people. So, for moderation's sake we say:—

"REACH FOR A LUCKY
INSTEAD OF A SWEET."

The Misses Catherine Moylan, Myrna Darby,
Murrel Finley, now appearing
in Ziegfeld's "Whoopee"

Myrna Darby

Catherine Moylan

Murrel Finley

Reach for a
Lucky instead of
a sweet.

LUCKY STRIKE
"IT'S TOASTED"
CIGARETTES

© 1929, The American
Tobacco Co., Manufacturers

"It's toasted" No Throat Irritation-
No Cough.

Coast to coast radio hook-up every Saturday night through the National Broadcasting Company's
network. The Lucky Strike Dance Orchestra in "The Tunes that made Broadway, Broadway."

This Lucky Strike ad designed to stimulate the purchase of cigarettes by women appeared in 1929. It delivered a double whammy by stirring up fears of being fat and ugly and offering hope of staying slender by substituting a smoke for a sweet, at the same time making it socially acceptable to do so by presenting the testimonials of three Ziegfeld stars, popular cultural heroines of the day.

increases date from World War I and continue to the present in spite of the banning of cigarette advertising from the electronic media.

The first advertising campaign directed to women and featuring women as smokers was launched by the American Tobacco Company for its Lucky Strike cigarettes in 1927. George Washington Hill explained in 1938:

> We never dared to talk about women smoking cigarettes, until what is known in the trade as the Lucky Strike campaign. We had a series of testimonials of opera singers, and among others was Madame Schumann-Heink. She was the first woman that ever publicly came out and testified that she smoked cigarettes, and she had rather an unpleasant experience. She was in the West and she had some dates with some girls' colleges to sing out there, and as soon as she published this she began to get cancellations of some of those dates, and she quit. But that was the start of the breaking down of the prejudice, and from that time on, of course, all cigarette manufacturers have developed all the romance they could use, using woman's testimonials and women in romantic situations.

The "testimonial" is a basic device in advertising, and usually the person testifying on behalf of the product is both famous and socially acceptable. Today we have testimonials from athletes, pop singers, actors and actresses, and many more hero types. In 1927, opera singers held the same interest and admiration for the general public as TV actors and ball players do today. Besides being famous, opera stars were socially acceptable at a time when dramatic and musical comedy stars were not.

The rapid increases in cigarette consumption dating from the late 1920s indicate that "creating a market" to increase the number of smokers played a bigger role in the growth of cigarette companies than did stimulating larger use per smoker. By exploiting a trend which sociologists say was already on the way because of the social changes that followed the end of World War II, the cigarette companies helped themselves.

Consider AT&T's institutional advertising campaign spotlighting social change within its organization. On pages 46–47 are two examples of the series, one of a handsome, contented looking young man with a mod haircut and sideburns working as a telephone operator, traditionally a woman's job, with a black woman operator next to him; the other, of a woman division manager, traditionally a man's job. Have you noticed any other ads of this type? For what purposes is the telephone company using these advertisements? Why does the telephone company, without any competition, advertise at all? What is "AT&T and your local Bell Company," who certainly don't need new customers, getting out of this?

What could be more socially acceptable than a bride smoking a cigarette? Notice the play on important words from the marriage ceremony, the bridal gown and veil to imply all the socially acceptable traditions of the large church wedding, the conservative hair style, the graceful and sophisticated pose of the model, who looks every inch a lady. What does all this say to a young woman debating the propriety of smoking? This ad ran in 1933.

Illustrations of Historic Ads

The advertisement for the Jordan Motor Car Company reproduced on page 48 is considered an advertising classic. It represents a milestone as well as a moment of change.

The Jordan was not a car in the same sense that the Ford is. Henry Ford invented his; Ned Jordan just bought parts from other manufacturers, had them put together in a small factory, then wrote wild, romantic ads to sell his cars. He was an advertising copywriter who had determined to make a fortune selling cars, and he did.

"West of Laramie" is one of the wildest and most romantic of Jordan's ads. When it appeared in *The Saturday Evening Post* on June 23, 1923, it had unusual impact. People talked about it, quoted it, tore it out to save. It was instrumental in changing the advertising "message," and anticipated the popularity of television's romantic Wild West. If today, "Somewhere

The phone company wants more division managers like Blanche Reardon.

Blanche Reardon is one of the several hundred women executives in the Bell System.

She is a Division Switching Manager for Illinois Bell. In that job she is responsible for the 506 men and women who maintain the equipment in 37 telephone exchanges in Chicago's southern suburbs.

Blanche began working for the phone company in 1954 in the Engineering Department. In the face of tough competition, she was promoted to various jobs in engineering and marketing. On the way up to Division Manager, she held such responsible positions as Transmission Systems Engineer and Data Marketing Manager.

What she wanted throughout her career was to have her work evaluated solely on merit. That was important.

And that's the way we want it throughout the Bell System. We want our people to do what they like to do and do best. And we want them to advance.

So today, when openings exist, local Bell Companies are offering applicants and present employees some jobs they may never have thought about before.

That's why in today's phone company you'll find both men and women working as mechanics, truck drivers, installers, operators, service representatives—and division managers.

AT&T and your local Bell Company are equal opportunity employers.

Courtesy, American Telephone and Telegraph

West of Laramie" consists of one major highway and miles and miles of nothing but miles and miles, do you think the Jordan Playboy could actually have been driven as illustrated in 1923? But that was unimportant as

The phone company wants more operators like Rick Wehmhoefer.

Rick Wehmhoefer of Denver, Colorado, is one of several hundred male telephone operators in the Bell System.

Currently, Rick is a directory assistance operator. "So far, my job has been pleasant and worthwhile," he says. "I enjoy assisting people."

We have men like Rick in a lot of different telephone jobs. Both men and women work as Bell System mechanics, truck drivers, installers and engineers.

We want the men and women of the telephone company to do what they want to do, and do best.

Today, when openings exist, local Bell Companies are offering applicants and present employees some jobs they may never have thought about before. We want to help all advance to the best of their abilities.

AT&T and your local Bell Company are equal opportunity employers.

Courtesy, American Telephone and Telegraph

the truth of the times is to the television Westerns. The important thing was that the ad sold cars.

The ad for the Ford Motor Company, which ran in *The Saturday*

Somewhere West of Laramie

SOMEWHERE west of Laramie there's a broncho-busting, steer-roping girl who knows what I'm talking about.

She can tell what a sassy pony, that's a cross between greased lightning and the place where it hits, can do with eleven hundred pounds of steel and action when he's going high, wide and handsome.

The truth is—the Playboy was built for her.

Built for the lass whose face is brown with the sun when the day is done of revel and romp and race.

She loves the cross of the wild and the tame.

There's a savor of links about that car—of laughter and lilt and light—a hint of old loves—and saddle and quirt. It's a brawny thing—yet a graceful thing for the sweep o' the Avenue.

Step into the Playboy when the hour grows dull with things gone dead and stale.

Then start for the land of real living with the spirit of the lass who rides, lean and rangy, into the red horizon of a Wyoming twilight.

JORDAN
JORDAN MOTOR CAR COMPANY, Inc., Cleveland, Ohio

Evening Post on October 3, 1908, was the first public announcement of the Model T Ford. Some 15,000,000 of them followed and literally created the Automobile Age, which we are now blessed and stuck with.

In the early toothpaste advertisement illustrated, the Pepsodent Company was selling beauty and romance. What are toothpaste ads selling today? How scientifically accurate were the ads then? How about now?

The Ivory soap advertisement was selling upward mobility, snob ap-

peal, appearance, popularity, and romance as these things were perceived in the early part of this century. What are soaps and detergents selling now?

Fear of illness and hope of health is still one of the strongest sellers of almost anything. The Health Jolting Chair illustrated was supposed to provide exercise without effort—a sales pitch that is still current. This ad dates from 1895.

Considering the increased use of cigarettes created by advertising,

Magic

Lies in pretty teeth—Remove that film

Why will any woman in these days have dingy film on teeth?

There is now a way to end it. Millions of people employ it. You can see the results in glistening teeth everywhere you look.

This is to offer a ten-day test, to show *you* how to beautify the teeth.

Film is cloudy

Film is that viscous coat you feel. It clings to the teeth, enters crevices and stays. When left it forms the basis of tartar. Teeth look discolored more or less.

But film does more. It causes most tooth troubles.

It holds food substances which ferment and form acid. It holds the acid in contact with the teeth to cause decay.

Germs breed by millions in it. They, with tartar, are the chief cause of pyorrhea.

Avoid Harmful Grit

Pepsodent curdles the film and removes it without harmful scouring. Its polishing agent is far softer than enamel. Never use a film combatant which contains harsh grit.

You leave it

Old ways of brushing leave much of that film intact. It

dims the teeth and, night and day, threatens serious damage. That's why so many well-brushed teeth discolor and decay. Tooth troubles have been constantly increasing. So dental science has been seeking ways to fight that film.

A new-type tooth paste has been perfected, correcting some old mistakes. These two film combatants are embodied in it. The name is Pepsodent, and by its use millions now combat that film.

Two other foes

It also fights two other foes of teeth. It multiplies the starch digestant in the saliva. To digest starch deposits on teeth which may otherwise cling and form acids.

It multiplies the alkalinity of the saliva. To neutralize mouth acids which cause tooth decay.

Lives altered

Whole lives may be altered by this better tooth protection. Dentists now advise that children use Pepsodent from the time the first tooth appears. It will mean a new dental era.

The way to know this is to send the coupon for a 10-Day Tube. Note how clean the teeth feel after using. Mark the absence of the viscous film. See how teeth whiten as the film-coats disappear.

See and feel the new effects, then read the reasons in the book we send.

Cut out the coupon now.

could increased use of soap have been stimulated in the same way? The Pears' soap ad shown appeared in the late nineteenth century.

The early cereal ad for Quaker Oats sold strength for young people by the "relationship" technique. Yesterday, "big circus acts." Today?

Marketing Techniques

You have seen how cigarette manufacturers doubled their sales by creating a new market of women smokers when their advertising took ad-

Linen is a more elegant material than cotton
for summer dress. Linen will look like
cotton if washed with any but Ivory Soap.

There is no "free" (uncombined) oil or alkali in Ivory Soap. The combination is complete. Containing no "free oil," it rinses perfectly. There being no "free alkali," it is harmless to color, skin or fabric. 99 44/100 per cent. pure. It floats.

The Health Jolting Chair

COPYRIGHT.

The most important Health Mechanism ever produced

A Practical Household Substitute for the Saddle-Horse.

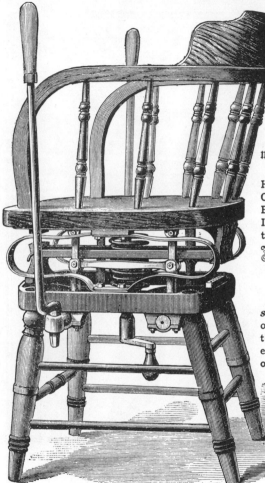

It affords a PERFECT means of giving EFFICIENT exercise to the ESSENTIALLY IMPORTANT NUTRITIVE ORGANS OF THE BODY in the most DIRECT, CONVENIENT, COMFORTABLE, and INEXPENSIVE manner.

Suitable for all ages and for most physical conditions.

INDISPENSABLE TO THE HEALTH AND HAPPINESS OF MILLIONS OF HUMAN BEINGS WHO MAY BE LIVING SEDENTARY LIVES through choice or necessity.

It preserves Health, cures Disease, and prolongs Life.

An *ingenious, rational, scientific, mechanical* means of overcoming those impediments to the taking of proper exercise, erected by the artificial methods of modern society.

For certain classes of invalids a veritable Treasure-Trove.

A CONSERVATOR of NERVOUS ENERGY.

No dwelling-house is completely furnished without The Health Jolting Chair.

vantage of existing, but slow-moving, forces of social change. You have seen how the telephone company reinforces its "good guy, progressive thinker" image by exploiting the current changes in attitude toward employment practices. Two more examples of creating markets will help you identify other trends currently in use by advertisers. Clothing manufac-

THE POWER TO DO EACH DARING FEAT
IN EACH BIG CIRCUS ACT
COMES FROM THE KIND OF FOOD THEY EAT—
FROM **Quaker Oats**
TO BE EXACT

turers created a market, first among teenage girls, then among women of all ages, for the sale of levis, dungarees, slacks, and trousers of all kinds after young girls had already started wearing boys' pants. Cosmetic manufacturers have created a market for hair spray among men of all ages who already used some sort of hair dressing.

Activity

Bring to class newspaper and magazine ads, as well as summaries or tape recordings of radio and television commercials, that are currently exploiting social change as a means of creating a market or reinforcing an image. What are the social changes currently taking place? Consider everyday habits of eating, dressing, marriage, education, and recreation that you take for granted. They may be changing, and you may be sure that advertising is accelerating the process.

Exploiting Age Groups

In addition to utilizing social change to sell products and reinforce images, advertisers consistently make use of a very old technique—divide and conquer.

People tend to clump into groups identified by common elements— age, sex, income, education, possessions, location, race—to name a few of the major determining factors. In spite of dire warnings by psychologists, physicians, sociologists, and other thoughtful people that emphasizing differ ences between groups leads to more bad effects than good, advertising enthusiastically plays upon these differences as a marketing technique.

Sociologists have suggested that advertising since World War II has so emphasized the normal conflict between generations that much more painful disruption in society has occurred than otherwise would have taken place. Advertisers found that affluent young people had money to spend and exploited that gold mine by emphasizing the idea that teenagers live in a world all their own. This idea was magnified, dressed up, and repeated frequently enough to establish the attitude that young people not only lived in a world of their own, separate and apart from the rest of humanity, but that it was an almost sacred world; therefore, young people had a right to repulse any efforts to control their spending. The most insidious part of the message was that spending money was "creative." What parent could be so cruel, retarded, and punitive as to psychologically damage the flowering of "creativity"? It was a very persuasive message, particularly successful in the affluent '50s and '60s. In this campaign, advertising was also assisted by psychological studies that revealed the internal and external forces that produce growth, development, and change in young people. By making use of this information to sell products, advertising helped exacerbate the tensions of the "generation gap," created a new market, and as a minor spin-off, helped some parents understand their growing children better. But the long term results seem to have made the distance between young people and their parents even greater.

To understand how advertisers make use of groups, look at the reproductions of ads for *Seventeen Magazine*. These ads are not directed to the general public, but to the advertisers themselves.

To what kind of audience will *Seventeen* guarantee to deliver the advertiser's message? A very specific market—girls 17 through 19 who are engaged. Such ads and others of their type appear regularly in trade publications within the media such as *Standard Rate and Data Service*, from which advertisers choose their publications and broadcasting outlets. From these sources, advertisers find not only space and time rates, but all the other information they need to place their specifically tailored material where it will do them the most good.

How do advertisers know what stimulates each group's hopes and fears? They use the findings of marketing research and the results of psychological studies. Some of these psychological studies, financed by and used almost entirely for advertising, are called "motivational research." These investigations identify the hopes and fears that, once stimulated, will motivate people to buy products. Other investigations of marketing research identify such factors as the age, sex, and income of an audience and identify specific groups within the audience. The "teen-aged market," "the young adult market between 18 and 35," "the prime bridal market," the "boys between 10 and 17 market," and all the other "markets" have been thoroughly researched so that advertising can be designed to create the response desired.

Advertisers are responsive to any public objection to their approach if not being responsive will cost them sales. If people become actively nonaccepting and unavailable to their message, advertisers look for the reasons. The sudden appearance, within eight months, of black people in print and electronic advertising was one response to a new, socially conscious attitude in America following the race riots in large cities triggered by Watts in 1965.

Another response to an unfavorable reaction was the quick disappearance of the cartoon character, the Frito Bandito, from Frit-O-Lay's potato and corn chip advertising. This withdrawal followed publication of a survey conducted by sociologists at California's Stanford University that revealed the resentment of Mexican-Americans to the promotion of an insulting image of themselves. The Frito Bandito was an animated-cartoon figure, short, fat, dressed in the large, droopy sombrero, serape, and baggy

The number 1 magazine from which teenage girls buy an advertised item.

Every issue of *SEVENTEEN* is read by half of the teenage girls of America. With 4 issues the total teen market is covered.

More brides-to-be buy *SEVENTEEN* than buy the bridal magazines.

SEVENTEEN readers are big spenders. They have two incomes going for them. One, from their families with incomes 54% greater than the national average. The other, from $8.7 billion a year of their own.

Teen girls represent 13% of the female population, yet they account for 23% of all apparel expenditures. (The total expenditure of teenage girls for apparel is $6.3 billion.) As to cosmetics and toiletries, these girls account for 20% of the total market expenditure.

SEVENTEEN reaches the vital first-time purchasers, more than any other magazine.

seventeen

Triangle Communications Inc.

320 Park Avenue
New York, N.Y. 10022
(212) 759-8100

Why you should be in the largest fashion magazine in the world.

The teenage girl (13-19) is the prime purchaser of all fashion in the U.S.A. today. They spent a grand total of $7.4 billion last year alone.

Every issue of *SEVENTEEN* is read by 7,000,000 teenage girls. More teenage girls than any other magazine.

SEVENTEEN readers are the big spenders. They have two incomes going for them. One, from their families with incomes 54% greater than the national average. The other, from $8.7 billion a year of their own.

SEVENTEEN gives you more Store Promotions. Over 14,000.

SEVENTEEN gives you more Retail Tie-in Linage. Over 3,500,000 lines.

SEVENTEEN gives you more circulation, 1,489,167, than any fashion magazine.

SEVENTEEN is the number one magazine from which teenage girls buy an advertised item.

For more information see the *SEVENTEEN* Tell-All (Class 49).

seventeen

Triangle Communications Inc.

320 Park Avenue
New York, N.Y. 10022
(212) 759-8100

Courtesy, Standard Rate and Data Services

pants that all Mexicans are supposed to wear, bearded and dirty, speaking
in a comic accent, who would steal all your chips if you didn't eat them
as soon as you bought them. It is easy to see why a self-respecting ethnic
group, with a proud heritage, would resent such a slur and object to the
use of such a misleading stereotype to sell products. (One of the worst
insults involved was that they were still supposed to buy the products!)
At the same time it should be noted that using stereotypes to illustrate
the so-called "average" successful person of an identified group, someone
you would want to imitate, is probably the major marketing technique
currently in use.

Activities

1. Drawing on our analysis of advertising so far, what other stereotypes can you recall? Start with the "average" housewife. What are the
elements of her advertising image?

How is the "average" man portrayed in ads and commercials? The
"average" high school student? The "average" engineer or physician?

Do you find these images admirable, insulting, or somewhere between? Why?

Can you find your own image in your group? What is your reaction
to it?

How does the use of these images tend to emphasize the differences
between groups? How could advertising emphasize the similarities of people in different groups?

2. Collect magazines that are directed to different audiences such as
teenaged girls and teenaged boys, affluent middle-aged women, affluent
middle-aged men, young men, young women, black people, sportsmen and
women, college educated people, and high-school educated people. Tear
out large ads for brand name products, being sure you write identification
on each.

Study these ads according to the analytical principles described and
practiced in the earlier part of this chapter. Decide which hopes and fears,
which words, and what art identify the audience for each advertisement.

Run the spliced films of commercials collected from the local television stations, stopping them as necessary to identify the audience for
which each was intended.

What hopes and fears of each audience are played upon? How do
they differ?

What ideal or average person is used for the members of the audience to imitate?

Which words appeal to which audience?

What marketing technique is used?

3. Either by voluntary choice or assignment, assume the role of advertisement producer for a *specific* audience. Choose a product and design an advertisement for print or a commercial for radio or television that will stimulate your specific audience to buy the product. Choose the hopes and fears you wish to play upon, the art you intend to use, and then organize the material into a whole.

Display your advertisement or commercial to the class so that they can decide if it appeals to the audience for which it was intended.

Consumer Protection

Although Federal laws, government agencies, and volunteer consumer organizations to protect the public have been in existence since the early 1900s, the buyer has always been the least protected person in town. One man, at the height of his exasperation with malfunctioning equipment, department store executives who ignored him, and a manufacturer whose guarantee didn't seem to guarantee anything, complained that a convicted murderer had more legal rights and ways to get help than a lawful citizen whose only crime was paying $1,000 for electrical appliances.

Because of increasing dissatisfaction with products that won't work properly or fall apart; with advertising made up of half truths, whole lies, and manipulative techniques; with faulty, misleading, or nonexistent information; and with tricky, fraudulent, and dishonest sales practices, people are demanding and, seemingly at last, beginning to get some real protection. New laws are being enacted with teeth in them that people hope will not prove to be false. New consumer offices, advisers, and representatives are being made part of county, state, and Federal governments, and the "consumer movement" or "consumerism" is starting to be taken seriously by manufacturers, wholesalers, and retailers who make up the business community. The balance of power as well as the advantages of certain traditional, if not legal, practices that the business community considers "rights" are still with the seller; however, real efforts are currently being exerted to equalize the "rights" of buyers.

Until recently, government and business operated on the idea that buyers had sufficient power and protection because they could decide not to buy. Sellers, therefore, could, more or less, set their own rules. Their rules, in the main, have been based on the centuries-old principle of *caveat emptor*, which means "let the buyer beware." This situation created a very intriguing game for sellers in which they could set the rules; tell buyers all, some, or none of them; and then, at will, change them.

Because of this underlying philosophy, sellers' *practices* have somehow over the years come to be thought of as their built-in, inherited *rights.* These include the right to introduce new products any time, in any size or shape, for any function or purpose, at any price, giving buyers whatever information and guarantees sellers considered adequate in their own interest, and to advertise and promote the product as much as, and in any way, they choose to stimulate as many sales as possible. In fact, marketing research flatteringly calls people who rush to buy new products "creative consumers," although objective observers have commented that "creative consumers" are more like spoiled children, demanding instant gratification. The immediate and supposedly adequate reply of the seller has been to say, "After all, buyers don't *have* to buy, do they?"

Contemporary consumerists do not consider the buyers' potential ability to refuse to buy adequate any more because of the powerful forces of both technology and advertising lined up against him. Advertising manipulates powerful psychological hopes and fears in an emotionally persuasive way, and technology has become so complex that buyers have neither full information about nor specialized, professional expertise in, for example, chemistry or electrical engineering, to name just two areas in which hard data is needed to make knowledgeable choices. To balance the "rights" of the seller, consumers are demanding "rights" such as adequate information about products, protection against faulty manufacture and questionable marketing practices, and the "right" to influence the creation of new products and the development of advertising and promotion practices that will enhance the "quality of life." This last item of the consumers' Bill of Rights is the radical one because it loosens the business community's control of the American way of life.

A majority of manufacturers of the nationally advertised brand-name products that we have been studying are outraged, hurt, and angry at consumer pressure. Some are hurt and angry because they thought, all along, that they had been honorably and adequately serving the public. Others are angry because of the threat of restraint. All are panicky at the threat of loss of profits—and the battle lines on the home front are, therefore, clearly drawn.

In the various skirmishes and major battles that consumer legislation and enforcement face, the business community can bring an arsenal of over a hundred years' investment of money and accumulation of power in Washington and state capital lobbies by the major business and manufacturing associations, not to mention the power and influence of giant corporations. Consumers have only one major weapon—numbers. The majority of people in this country are involved, whether they know it or not. The majority can wield overwhelming power, should they ever make an effort to do so. In addition, the tide of history seems to be running with consumers, primarily for two reasons—the increasing education and affluence of people and their awareness of the danger to the world's resources. These two reasons seem to be influencing political leaders and some farsighted members of the business community into a pro-consumer outlook.

The farsighted businessmen who see the value of consumerism say they have to figure out ways of doing several things simultaneously. They have to find ways to satisfy the demands of the public for immediate, or short-term, satisfaction while enhancing the long-term quality of life. For example, large, flashy cars with powerful motors please their owners (short-term satisfaction) but increase pollution, traffic congestion, difficulty of parking, and the danger of accidents because of speed; therefore, they reduce the long-term quality of life.

In a way, manufacturers' problems are similar to those of parents trying to rear healthy children. Children would prefer to eat only candy, potato chips, hamburgers, fries, and milk shakes, which satisfy their immediate tastes, but wise parents know that, in the long run, such a diet is harmful to their health. But how do you convince a child that vegetables must be eaten before the candy? Parents can insist in a variety of ways, but a manufacturer would go out of business if products that were "good for" people did not sell. However, the number of farsighted businessmen among manufacturers and retailers is a mere fraction of the majority, and the majority seem more interested in immediate, short-term satisfactions, such as profits, than in long-term enhancement of the "quality of life," even for their own families. Therefore, the battle to increase consumer protection and thereby counterbalance traditional sellers' practices will probably continue for some time.

Gains brought about by recent drives for consumer protection laws and their enforcement include the following: A Truth-in-Lending Law, Truth-in Packaging Law, Child Protection and Toy Safety Act, Fair Credit Reporting Act, and Auto Safety Law.

A Federal Office of Consumer Affairs and an Environmental Protection Agency have been created, and both the Federal Trade Commission and Federal Food and Drug Administration have been strengthened.

Reaction in individual states has ranged from increased staffing and support of Consumer Advisors offices to virtually their abolition. What will happen in the future in both state and national governments will depend upon the philosophy of the incumbent administration.

Activities

1. By searching through the local libraries, the telephone book, and state and county directories, discover what governmental consumer offices and volunteer organizations exist in your part of the country. What are these governmental offices and organizations designed to do? What areas do they cover? What are their limitations? What methods of public edu-

cation are they using? How effective are these methods? What legal powers
do they have?

2. By volunteer choice or assignment, decide upon one of the following organizations, or a division within it, and explore its history. Discover
how it came into being, its purpose, its support and power to enforce acts
and laws, and what products in what areas of life it is concerned with:

President's Committee on Consumer Interests
Federal Trade Commission (multiple divisions)
Consumer and Marketing Service, U.S. Department of Agriculture
Food and Drug Administration (multiple divisions)
National Bureau of Standards, Department of Commerce
Interstate Commerce Commission
Securities and Exchange Commission
Alcohol and Tobacco Tax Division, Department of the Treasury
Administration on Aging, Department of Health, Education and Welfare
ENACT groups
Product Safety Commission
Better Business Bureau
Consumer's Union
National Consumers League
Nader's Public Interest Research Group

3. *A Consumer Case History to Consider*   Gather the following
items to examine: (a) *Consumer Reports*, March 1971 issue, p. 139; and
(b) American Tourister Luggage advertisement in *Newsweek*, June 19, 1972
issue, or any thereafter that shows a piece of luggage holding a heavy
weight or being thrown from a great height.

When Consumer's Union published the report of its tests of the luggage on page 139 of its March 1971 issue of *Consumer Reports*, American
Tourister threatened to sue, not on the basis that their advertisement was
true and could be proved so in court, but on the basis of technical details
of the test. American Tourister did not take the case to court, but they
modified their ads, as you can see. This little story raises several questions.
One of them should be about the differences between the original ad that
caused Consumer's Union to test the luggage and the subsequent, modified
ads. What are the differences? Are they enough to change the main thrust
of this particular advertising campaign,

Another question this case history should raise concerns consumerism
as a whole. How valuable is it? Suppose the luggage company had taken
Consumer's Union to court. Would the resulting drain of money, time,
and effort been worth it to the Union? How would other consumer
agencies have reacted, do you imagine? Have other cases of this type been
reported? What were the conclusions?

THE IMPACT OF ADVERTISING

4. Investigate *The New York Times Index, The Newspaper Index,* and the *Reader's Guide to Periodical Literature* to discover the current status of the following items. If there is nothing in the news about them, try other sources such as the local office of the Federal agency responsible.

(a) Efforts by the National Bureau of Standards to persuade the clothing industry to use the same measurements for garments.

(b) The Federal Trade Commission's efforts to persuade food and drug manufacturers to correct false nutritional claims for either increased energy or weight reduction in advertising.

(c) Efforts by the Food and Drug Administration to inform the public of fakes and swindles. Information on this subject can be found among Government documents in libraries.

(d) The Federal Trade Commission's challenges of false advertising claims for pain-killers.

(e) Ralph Nader's efforts to persuade the government to reform the national Civil Service.

(f) The Food and Drug Administration's efforts to persuade bicycle manufacturers to use safety standards for bike designs.

(g) Status of the proposed Consumer Protection Agency legislation, which Congress has had under consideration for close to five years.

(h) The Federal Trade Commission's requests that toothpaste manufacturers substantiate their advertising claims.

(i) Any new challenges, test cases, or legislation currently in the news.

Chapter 4
Format of Contemporary Media

The mass media make it possible today for you to be a member of the best informed public in history. However, since the invention of the first mass medium, the newspaper, almost three centuries ago, a continuing debate has been carried on, by everyone who has an interest in what the public thinks and does, about whether the information so received is the whole truth, half-truth, or no truth at all. This debate became particularly intense during the growth to gianthood of radio and television, because air waves, unlike print, have from the beginnings of broadcasting been considered public property.

Before you can judge the "truth" of the matter, you must see clearly the foundation upon which the structure of contemporary media has been built.

The two foundation stones are money and political influence. Although journalism has made major contributions to society and will, no doubt, continue to do so, these two goals have motivated media growth and production from their beginnings. The public welfare is served so long as the media are served also. When political power and wealth have been achieved in such abundance that serving the public is possible without threat or loss, educational programs, service to democratic processes, and humane purposes are provided by and through the media. When either profit or political power is threatened, programs and policies that serve the public interest are decreased or discontinued.

The passive person who goes through life without questioning how, why, or to what end anything is done usually believes not only advertising claims, but also the media's public relations policies; he thereby willingly provides the responses predetermined for anothers' benefit, with the idea, no doubt, that the service he receives is worth the price. Therefore, the questions you need to ask yourself constantly are "What is the price? Is it worth the return?"

Of the two foundation stones—money and politics—influencing political action was primary when mass media began in this country in the 1600s. As newspapers and magazines became independent businesses in the 1800s, the need to make money to survive as a business, then to show a profit, combined with, and occasionally superseded, the desire to influence. In the era of the Robber Barons, political exposés in the public interest contributed greatly to journalism's financial profit and political power.

The growth of newspapers and magazines created whole new professions in the late 1800s and early 1900s. Reporters and editors who were not also type setters and printers were the forerunners of professional Schools of Journalism. News photography grew and developed as a distinct profession as the technical processes of film making, developing, printing, and transmitting pictures advanced. The technology of mass printing and its various trades stemmed from the development of the rotary press for faster printing of newspapers in the mid-1800s. At that time, journalism's desire to become a respected part of the community turned the attention of politically powerful and financially secure newspaper owners to the development of an organized profession. Today the media as a whole constitute a massive and intricate industrial complex, mostly owned by giant corporations who control a huge diversity of intertwined merchandising, governmental, and military interests. Their general policies require media production that will maintain and increase both financial and political profit.

Although this text cannot provide a detailed history of either print or broadcasting journalism, a brief survey of the high points—events that brought about changes in the direction or control of the media's growth, and key personalities who were vivid, adventuresome, and inventive people— should help you evaluate the information-giving aspect of the media as you have already evaluated the entertainment and advertising aspects. Standard histories of journalism and broadcasting are readily available for those whose curiosities will be stirred to investigate in greater detail. Please note before you go to the library, however, that most of these books can be divided into two groups, one whose attitude is "Oh, aren't the media wonderful!" and the other, "Oh, aren't the media dreadful!" You will have to provide a balanced viewpoint for yourself.

The following exercises will prepare you for a look at the turning points in the media's growth by acquainting you with the format of each medium, as well as the similarities and differences of the various types of contemporary journalism. The following chapters will document the pattern-setting days of both the print and electronic media.

Activities

For the following assignments, the class can divide into groups, each group to work on a specific medium, or each student can do a shortened version of each assignment for each medium.

1 Format

A.   Bring to class a recent issue of the newspaper that your family reads. Choose a date either by consensus of the class or assignment by the instructor because, for this activity, it is necessary for each student to have a paper of the same date. Make sure that both small town and metropolitan dailies are represented. The school library can be helpful here, if necessary.

Answer the following questions either orally or in writing. If this is a written assignment, first set up a sheet of paper with the following headings:

SECTION NUMBER AND NAME
FIRST PAGE SUBJECTS
OTHER SUBJECTS

For example, Section I of almost every newspaper consists of national and international news. What else does it contain?

(1) What is the major news event headlined in the largest type on each front page? Is it the same for every paper of that date? What are the differences?

(2) In newspapers in which the major headlines are about the same event, is there any difference in wording? If so, what is it? What is the purpose of each wording?

(3) Which paper or papers use "scare" headlines? Which headlines prove misleading when you read into the material? What do these devices in headline writing do for the paper?

(4) Where and what is the major local story? Is it handled in the same way that national and international coverage is handled?

(5) What does the position in the paper of an item tell about its importance?

(6) How many and what kinds of pictures are used? How does each relate to the material it illustrates?

B.   Watch the major television newscasts starting at 6 P.M. and those starting at 10, 10:30, or 11 P.M. Each network and independent station in the area should be monitored on an assigned or voluntary basis. Bring these observations to class to combine with your observations on newspaper format.

Use the form shown for each telecast that you observe. When you copy it (or if someone types a ditto for the whole class), leave sufficient room under Items Broadcast for a longer list than the space here indicates. The notes under 1, 2, and 3 are informational only.

Television Newscast Format

Channel No. and Call Letters ———— Network ———— Date and Time ————

Name of leading personality ——————————————————————

Name of program ——————————————————————

Items Broadcast	*Characteristics Displayed by Leading Personality*
————————————	————————————
————————————	————————————
————————————	————————————

Record the frequency of the following techniques by making slash marks as each appears. Total at end.

(1) Number of film clips used: ———————— Total: ————————
(Note: A "film clip" is a still photograph that appears behind or to the side of the screen while the reporter talks in the foreground. It's done by use of two or more cameras.)

(2) Number of remotes and tape inserts used: ———— Total: ————
(Note: A "remote" is a direct broadcast from the scene with a reporter ad-libbing a description or reading one prepared before he went to the scene to be filmed. A "tape insert" is a video tape recording taken at the scene for use later. A viewer can't tell much difference between them.)

(3) Number of studio interviews used: ———————— Total: ————————
(Note: A "studio interview" brings a person involved in an event or issue into the studio to be interviewed by a reporter while on the air.)

Number the list of "Items Broadcast." Under "Characteristics," list the mannerisms as you see them. Include appearance. Remember, though, that everyone on camera wears make-up.

Once you have recorded all this information, answer the following questions:

(1) Assuming that the first few items on the newscast correspond in importance to those on the newspaper's front page, what were the top stories? Were they the same for each 6 o'clock newscast on every station? What were the differences?

(2) Compare the Items Broadcast for each newscast in the same time slot. In what ways are the newscasts similar in format? In what ways are they different? Are there more differences than similarities?

(3) Compare the characteristics of the leading personality of each newscast. What "image" does each project? Who does that particular image

resemble in the local population? What impact does this similarity have on local viewers?

(4) Are the images of the individual newscasters essentially different or similar?

(5) What factors create the loyalty of its audience to each news program? What causes you to make your choice of programs? If it's your parents' choice, why do they choose that one program?

C.   Bring to class issues of weekly news magazines that provide news coverage for the dates of both the papers and telveision newscasts that you analyzed. Keeping your newspaper observations and Television Newscast Format beside your magazine, determine whether or not the magazine follows the same or a different basic format. Measure the proportion of advertising to information space in the same way you did for newspapers.

Conclusions about Format

(1) On the basis of the foregoing collection of data, what general conclusions can you make about how journalism in the media is organized?

(2) What are the major sections for the presentation of information? What purpose does the placement of each serve?

(3) What are the major differences and the major similarities among the media? Are there more differences or more similarities?

(4) What is NOT reported that would be interesting or important to know?

(5) What is reported too much and thus could be cut down or even eliminated?

Conclusions about Space and Time Allocations

As a result of the empirical evidence tabulated in the foregoing survey and the evidence tabulated in the Activities in Chapter 3, what conclusions can you reach about the amount of space available for news and other information on specific days in the print media? About the amount of time available in the electronic media?

Based on the amount of time and space available, what guides the editors in selection of the information to be used?

After comparing the run of stories in the prominent positions in the newspapers and television newscasts, how much variety does the average reader and viewer receive?

2   *Special Project*

Using all the information you have gathered and the conclusions you have reached in the foregoing assignments, prepare a multi-media documentary using one of the following subjects or one of your own devising: "Today's News Coverage Situation," "Superiority of Newspaper Reporting Over That of TV," "Superiority of TV Reporting Over That of Newspapers."

You might consider developing and presenting a story of the type NOT found in any of the media. As materials, you can use still photographs from newspapers and magazines, taped interviews with people on campus who can respond to questions you set up in advance, coverage of a campus or local event by motion picture camera, and narration to hold the segments together.

A newspaper makes the multitude too familiar with the actions and councils of their superiors and gives them not only an itch but a kind of colorable right and license to be meddling with the government.

Roger L'Estrange
Licenser of the Press
London, England, 1680

*Congress shall make no law . . .
abridging the freedom of the press.*

Art. I, First Amendment
United States Constitution
November 3, 1791

Courts officially ordered American newspapers not to publish [the Pentagon papers] because these materials offended the government . . .

Ben H. Bagdikian
The Effete Conspiracy

Chapter 5
Pattern-Setting in Print Media

Advance Preparation

1. Bring to class newspapers covering several consecutive days or use the ones saved from the Format and Space Allocation studies.

2. Arrange with newspapers for editors and reporters to speak about their jobs. Try to have people from newspapers of conflicting political affiliations. Have questions prepared in advance based on data you have collected about journalism in the media.

3. If the speakers will give permission, tape their comments for study and comparison. You might store the tapes in the school library so that future classes may compare past with present.

4. Schedule a film about collecting news and/or the organization and functioning of a newspaper or electronic news department either before or after the speakers. A film prepared as publicity usually puts an organization's best foot forward to present an ideal. A speaker, if questioned, can tell you the day-to-day workings of that ideal. Look and listen for differences and similarities between the ideal and the reality.

The activities you performed in foregoing chapters taught you the basic format and basis of space/time allocations in the media today. You probably were aware, generally, of the evidence you gathered without ever having conducted such a detailed examination, but you now have specific data to support your general impressions. Let's now consider the high points and key personalities in the pattern-setting days of the print medium's growth to institutional status.

History of Newspapers

Publishing in the United States has a tradition as long as the country's history because this continent was colonized after the invention of the printing press. Our forbears brought with them not only presses, but the books, newspapers, and magazines that were part of their lives in Europe. In addition, every ship from Europe brought its supply of printed materials to people eagerly waiting for the news. It was a bit old—six months to two years—but nonetheless of vital importance to the colonists.

Agitation for a "free press," that is, no control by government on the product of a printing press, had been going on long before we became a nation. For example, John Milton, the great Puritan poet and propagandist, wrote a pamphlet in England in 1644 protesting Parliamentary censorship. He said, "Give me the freedom to know, to utter and to argue freely, according to conscience, above all liberties." We, therefore, inherited a strong desire for the ideals written into the Constitution's Bill of Rights. Putting these ideals into day-to-day practice, however, is still an unfulfilled promise.

Because we were originally colonized as a commercial extension of a government based upon inherited power, we had to break away from Great Britain even to start the process toward the ideals of democratic freedom. Long before the actual break, however, printers and printing presses were at work. Printer Benjamin Harris published in 1690 in Boston the first issue of a native newspaper, *Publick Occurrences Both Foreign and Domestick*. It wasn't really much of a newspaper, but it was the first. All the foreign "news" was six months to two years old, editorial comment was not marked as such, and the ads were simple announcements of where products and services were available, with promises of satisfaction.

Among the many printer-publishers who flourished in the colonies during the eighteenth century, Benjamin Franklin is probably the best known. His brother, James, started *The Daily Courant* in 1721 in Boston as a minor aspect of his printing business because James and a group of friends were interested in politics. When Benjamin was apprenticed to his brother to learn how to be a printer, the statesman-scientist-to-be set type, printed the sheets by hand on a flat-bed press, and then, as he recorded in his *Autobiography*, "I was employed to carry the papers through the streets to the customers." He also wrote articles under an assumed name and, later, when James was jailed for publishing information in the *Courant* that the governor objected to, Benjamin continued publication of the paper.

Throughout the 1700s and well into the middle of the 1800s, the cost of publishing a newspaper was paid for by profits from other kinds of printing. A paper was usually published because of the political interests of the publisher and his friends. Some publishers printed the information that the government wished them to; some did not. Publishers who criticized the government's actions or the governor's behavior—each colony, particularly Massachusetts Bay, had some degree of autonomy as long as the money flowed from America to Britain—got into trouble, with jail sentences and confiscation of their presses the standard punishments.

Whether or not newspapers—and by extension, radio and television—have the right to publish information that the government does not wish published has been a controversial question for centuries. It still is. Even with the *legal* right now established by specific law, the question of how much information is to be provided to whom, in what form, and at what time, is debated under other vocabularies. The standard phrases used to withhold, slant, or falsify information are "to protect the security of the country," the necessity for "managed news," and the need for "interpretive reporting." The latter two are based upon the assumption that the average person cannot understand nor evaluate the great volume of information pertaining to any given issue or situation. Protecting the "security of the country" can be and has been used to cover a multitude of matters. "Managed news" was President John Kennedy's phrase after the Bay of Pigs fiasco; "interpretive reporting" is the media's own invention.

Comments in news articles such as "The bill passed the House and was sent to the Senate where it will probably die in committee" used to be considered editorializing because they contain opinion. These comments and others like them, even in news articles without the writer's name given, are now called "interpretive reporting." Journalists justify these comments by saying that the general public needs both the background material and the "educated prediction of events" to form personal opinions. Many thoughtful people claim that this kind of comment belongs on the editorial page.

Others call it propaganda because its purpose is to lead readers to support the politics of the newspaper or network.

Back in the mid-1730s, the first successful break-away of the newspapers from complete governmental control was made possible by the Zenger trial decision.

John Peter Zenger was a printer-publisher whose paper was only one aspect of his printing business. He wasn't as excited about politics as many others of his time, but he agreed to create a test case. His *New York Weekly Journal* published criticism of William Cosby, governor of New York, in the face of repeated orders to stop. Zenger was jailed, tried for criminal libel, and in 1736, acquitted.

The trial is considered the start of our traditional "freedom of the press," and the actual decision was both specific and specifically enduring. It set two precedents that survive in law today. One is that truth is a "complete defense" of libel. In other words, printed derogatory statements are not libel if they are true, and the publisher or author can prove that they are true. If a publisher or an author does not have evidence that will stand up in court, then he can be subject to large damage payments. The second precedent, therefore, is that newspapers *can* criticize the government subject to this definition of libel.

The result of Zenger's trial was not a leap into nonpartisan, objective political reporting. Quite the contrary. It loosened governmental control, as well as officials' whimsical interpretation of libel so that the political activists could be more outspoken than ever before, and political propaganda was consistently printed as "news." Propaganda is a dirty word if you are on the other side, whatever the other side may be. In the hands of John Adams, Thomas Paine, Thomas Jefferson, George Washington, Patrick Henry, James Madison, Alexander Hamilton, and the other Founding Fathers, both the political propaganda printed as "news" and the outright political propaganda such as Paine's *Common Sense*, that helped swing public sentiment to favor the Declaration of Independence, and the Madison-Hamilton-Jay *Federalist Papers*, that achieved ratification of the Constitution, are part of the foundation of our country and the democratic ideals of our government.

From pre-Revolutionary days to the mid-1800s, every newspaper was in the owner's complete control. The cost of publication was paid for by his printing business and maybe a little something from his political friends. The owner's political allegiance dictated the contents of the newspaper's political articles and editorial commentary.

Every newspaper usually stated openly which political party it supported, and the printer-owner, hired editor, and politically active friends of the printer wrote the "news" accordingly. If a paper supported a member of Congress, for example, any speech he made was reported as "full of stirring phrases, strong and courageous as a lion facing his multitudinous enemies, patriotism ringing in every tone of his voice. . . ." The paper against him would report the same speech as "foolhardy to the point of imbecility. In urging this specious action upon the country, Mr. Soandso displayed not only lack of reason and responsible caution, but an enthusiasm for disaster that labels him TRAITOR!" Libel was frequent and part of the daily game of politics, but politicians and their friends were wary of filing suit both because all sides were equally guilty of the same practice and most of the name-calling was not taken seriously, and because of actual truths that might be revealed in court.

Activities

1   Political Reporting—News and Opinion

Generally, a newspaper's political allegiance is known today by the comments and recommendations made for, against, and about political issues and candidates on the editorial pages. The news pages are supposed to report the issues objectively, from a nonpartisan standpoint. Do they? The following activities will show you what to look for in order to answer that question accurately.

A.   Locate an article about a currently important national political issue which was commented upon on the same date in each paper represented in the class collection. Notice the location of the article and the headline size. If it is about a Democrat or an issue the Democrats are supporting, does the location, size, and wording of the headline reflect the paper's political allegiance? Does the headline include words of approval or disapproval which clue you in on the paper's stand on the issue? Does a known Democratic paper play up the issue more favorably than a Republican paper, or vice versa?

B.   Does the article have a by-line? The "by-line" gives either the name and organization of the writer or only his name and is placed between the headline and "dateline" (the place of origin and date preceding the first sentence of the article itself). Who is the writer? Is his or her name well known to the general public? Who does the writer work for? If there is no by-line, who wrote the article? How can you find out? How do you know if the information is accurate? Is the article a piece of publicity, propaganda, or real news?

C.   Now look at the dateline. Do you see any initials, either within or without parentheses, after the place of origin and date, if the latter is used? The initials could be AP for Associated Press; UPI, United Press International; NANA, North American Newspaper Alliance; INS, Intercity News Service; Chicago Tribune-New York Times Syndicate; Los Angeles Times Syndicate; or some other group, chain, or newspaper combination. If it is an article from Washinton, New York, or any other place that the people involved in this political issue might be in for the moment, how many different initials are represented in the papers you have in class? How many viewpoints are you getting about this important national political issue?

D.   Read through the first two or three paragraphs of the article. What are the differences and similarities in the wording? What descriptive words are used, such as adjectives, for the people, legislation, or point in conflict? Do these words trigger emotions of approval or disapproval?

E.   Check through the editorial pages of several issues of your newspaper whose dates follow the publication of the article you are investigating. Check the signed political columns and cartoons that your paper carries, as well as the paper's own editorials. The editorials are traditionally run down the left side of the page in double- or triple-column widths and in type a size larger than that of the rest of the paper. Collect the editorial columns and cartoons concerning the issue, then compare them with the news reports from the news pages. What are the differences and similarities between the news and the opinions? Are the key words of description, such as adjectives for people and adverbs for their actions, the same in both news and opinions? The emotion-triggering words used in both news and opinion, as well as in advertising, are the clues to the predetermined response the originators of this information desire from you.

Conclusions about Political Reporting

On the basis of your close examination of all aspects of the information you have received about this important political issue of national politics which can be considered typical of all, answer the following questions either in writing or orally

(1) Are news and opinion kept separate in political newspaper reporting?

(2) Is there evidence of "interpretive reporting" in the news articles?

(3) Were there several viewpoints represented?

(4) Was material omitted that might influence your opinion on the issue?

(5) Are you satisfied with the depth of newspaper coverage of this issue and, by extension, of their coverage of politics in general?

(6) Is there too much political reporting? Not enough?

(7) What suggestions can you make about political reporting for the future?

2   *Opinion and Debate Question*
What are your reactions to the cartoon shown on the following page, in which a member of Congress, identified by his tie and briefcase, and the sketch of the Capitol building in the background, replies to a question by a member of *Small Society*, you and me?

History of News Gathering

Although political news was not the only news printed in the past, it was, as it is now, the most important. For the rest, publishers and editors accepted whatever information came to them. They printed verses, essays, prayers, sermons, homilies, notices of visiting relatives, gossip—anything offered was used to fill out the pages. Except for political information, no one connected with a newspaper went anywhere to gather news until about 1811. A young Bostonian named Samuel Topliff, Jr., is credited with starting the journalistic push-and-shove technique of news gathering. Topliff was employed to keep up handwritten ledgers, called News Books, in the Reading Room of the Exchange Coffee House. Coffee house owner Samuel Gilbert had started these News Books as a promotional device to attract customers. He succeeded so well that his enthusiastic customers gave him a rowboat in which to meet incoming ships for the news that he wrote into his Books. Between his growing coffee house business and keeping up with the information brought to him, Gilbert became so busy that he needed help and hired Topliff to maintain the Books.

Topliff's moment in history arrived on a dark, stormy night in November, 1811. A lookout ran in, wet and panting, to report an unidentified boat trying to cross Boston Harbor. The news caused an uproar among coffee house patrons. Danger from the British, danger from pirates, danger of some sort was the immediate reaction. To prevent a riot of fear on the basis of no information, and at much danger to himself in such weather, Topliff rowed into the harbor. He returned with the following information: The brig, *Latona*, was an American ship whose captain told of being boarded by men from a British sloop-of-war trying to pirate seamen into their Navy, and the British officer claimed that his country's entire Navy was on its way to retake the American colonies for England. It wasn't completely true, of course, but pirating American seamen was one of the reasons for the War of 1812. The significance to journalism of Topliff's rowboat trip was that it led to frequent boat races in all ports between reporters of competing papers to meet incoming ships to gather the news.

The political "party press" began to lose strength in the 1840s. Newspapers in all major cities were growing in strength, importance, power, and independence as newspaper publishing became a business in its own right, not just an adjunct of a printing company. Many publishers maintained printing companies, but these were no longer considered the same as newspaper printing. This change came about both because of the growth of advertising and the emergence of the publisher as businessman. Until approximately the end of World War I, being able to write was not considered special, unique, nor difficult, except for poetry. It was something every educated person could do; therefore, anyone who entered the newspaper business in any capacity was capable of writing well. This attitude lasted well into the twentieth century. Toward the end of the nineteenth century, however, although the same person was frequently publisher, editor, and reporter, increasingly the businessman and the reporter became two separate people. The businessman-owner remained boss.

The growth of advertising in the mid-1800s shifted financial support of the news pages from other printing contracts that had nothing to do with the number of people who read the paper to support from advertisers whose use of a paper depended entirely upon the number of people who read it. At the same time, newspapers expanded their coverage to appeal to larger numbers of people by including "human interest" material such as personality sketches of important local and national figures, divorce and murder trial stories, and reports of crime and other disasters. For information of this sort, reporters hung around police stations and courtrooms where they were not considered socially nor officially acceptable by anyone. However, from these murky beginnings, the highly respected "police beat" developed to such a point that today the attorneys for charged and sometimes convicted criminals, murderers to shoplifters, will call newspapers and offer to hold a "press conference." More often, though, particularly in juicy divorce cases and murder trials, reporters have to be dodged by the people involved, if talking to the press does not appear to them to help their case.

Divorce case reporting and police reports first appeared in *The New York Sun*, which Benjamin Day founded in 1833. Other papers quickly imitated the *Sun* because of the popularity of these reports. Such efforts to sell newspapers in ever larger numbers to readers and advertisers by emphasizing crime and disaster reporting were so successful that they grew into the traditional coverage found in all media today.

In 1835, James Gordon Bennett started *The New York Herald* and became one of the key personalities and innovators of the journalism of the mid-1800s. Described as a pugnacious Scot with a squint, his competitive

James Gordon Bennett, one of the giants of the newspaper business
in the nineteenth century (from a contemporary engraving).

drive, energy, fearlessness, economic shrewdness, and ability to learn from
experience made him a leader in this new business of running newspapers.
His paper was not the first of its kind, but it became one of the best.

The New York Herald provided a greater variety of local coverage,
better foreign news, more news of theatrical events, a higher degree of political independence (his editorials supported no political party at first although he later backed the Democrats), and better Wall Street reports than
any other paper could offer. Bennett himself wrote what he called "the
money article" because his college work had been in economics, and he had
had experience as a teacher and lecturer on the subject. His work in this
field formed the basis of the modern financial section.

The Herald carried an early version of today's society section and also reported sports events. Bennett hired correspondents in foreign cities and on our own Western Frontier. Later he sent his own reporters to Washington, Europe, Mexico—wherever events were happening that made news. He hired a fleet of boats in New York harbor to intercept the trans-Atlantic steamers bringing him the news from Europe so that he could get it printed and on sale before the other papers had a chance. He was also one of the founders of the Associated Press. His methods of covering the Mexican War and reporting the firing on Fort Sumter put *The Herald's* circulation ahead of all the other New York papers.

Bennett was not always liked nor respected, although even his detractors admitted his abilities. After *The Herald* had become a major success and Bennett himself wealthy and influential, he got drunk on the idea of his own power and wrote much that was foolish and bombastic. However, his impact on journalism remains influential today, and accounts of his adventurous and flamboyant personality are material for several books.

Horace Greeley, another influential journalist who became a political leader aspiring to the presidency, started *The New York Tribune* in 1841. His staff included many of journalism's nineteenth century greats, including Henry J. Raymond, one of the founders of *The New York Times* in 1851; Charles A. Dana, who took over *The Sun* in 1868; Whitelaw Reid, who took over *The Tribune* in 1872; and Margaret Fuller, literary editor and a leader of the Women's Lib of the 1800s, who later affiliated with *The Atlantic Monthly Magazine*.

Ms. Fuller was not the first woman in early journalism—wives and widows of early printers had always been active in their husbands' work, the wives setting type and doing some writing, the widows carrying on the whole business—but she was one of the most distinguished. Cornelia Walter edited the *Boston Transcript* between 1842 and 1847; Anne Royal, the weekly *Paul Pry* in Washington; Jane Grey Swisshelm, the Pittsburgh *Saturday Visitor* from 1848 to 1852. Ms. Swisshelm later became Washington correspondent for her own paper and the *New York Tribune*. Sara Willis Parton, under the name of Fanny Fern, became a famous contributor to the New York *Ledger*.

The great New York papers—the *Sun, Herald, Tribune,* and *Times*—led the way into what we now know as professional journalism. One by one, the various functions involved in running newspapers were separated into distinct departments, managed by people other than editors and reporters. Once a paper was an established business and making a profit, the publisher could use his political influence, backed by his financial power and direct access to the public, as he wished. Napoleon is supposed to have said, "Four hostile newspapers are more to be feared than a thousand bayonets." And

Thomas Carlyle, an important British writer who lived during the time newspapers were building their influence, wrote, "Great is Journalism. Is not every able editor a Ruler of the World, being a persuader of it?"

While the Eastern papers, particularly those in New York, Boston, and Philadelphia, were becoming large, successful business enterprises and setting the pace in professional journalism, the population was moving west. In each small settlement, the story goes, the saloon opened first, the jail next, then the newspaper when a vagabond printer with "a shirt-tail full of type" sobered up. Unfortunately, the itinerant and probably alcoholic printers, some of them very competent when sober, gave reporters the reputation of being habitual drunks. This reputation has survived so far into the twentieth century that even a contemporary woman reporter is almost automatically offered a drink by news sources at eight in the morning or later as an inducement or reward for writing a story.

There were enough of those vagabond printers who liked their booze to create the folktale; however, they were not usually the ones who established the papers, kept them running on a profitable basis, and became powerful enough figures in their own area to help establish the government, achieve statehood, decide about slavery, and take part in the national government.

The following list is provided to illustrate how early in the nineteenth century many influential Western papers were started. Read it to martial music, featuring trumpet fanfares and drums. As your eye goes from line to line, you will be able to hear the creak of wagon wheels and John Wayne declaring between bullets, "Nothin's gonna stop this country movin' West!" It's a pageant of THE PROGRESS WEST.

This list covers just the first half of the century because those were the pattern-setting days of the print medium. After 1865, the increased dependence on advertising, consolidation of several papers into one, incorporation and the resulting "big business" attitude, development of nonpartisan political reporting, and increased professionalism of editors and reporters were all signs that papers in the West were following the lead of the papers in large Eastern cities.

> 1813—Nacogdoches (Texas) *El Mejicano*, in Spanish.
> 1815—Cincinnati (Ohio) *Gazette*. By the 1850s, Cincinnati supported eight to ten dailies.
> 1833—Chicago (Illinois) *Weekly Democrat*. Later a daily and politically powerful.
> 1834—Taos (New Mexico) *El Crepusculo*, in Spanish.
> 1835—San Felipe (Texas) *Telegraph and Texas Register*. Official voice of the revolutionary government when Texas was fighting Mexico.

1836—Dubuque (Iowa) *Visitor.*

1837—Milwaukee (Wisconsin) *Sentinel.*

1837—New Orleans (Louisiana) *Picayune.* A *picayune* was a coin worth six and a quarter cents, which became the price of the paper.

1844—Tahlequah (Oklahoma Indian Territory) *The Cherokee Advocate.* Published by the Cherokee Baptist Mission, *The Advocate* was more a religious pamphlet than a newspaper; it was bilingual, using a Cherokee alphabet.

1846—Oregon City (Oregon) *Spectator.*

1847—Santa Fe (New Mexico) *Republican.* Two pages in English; two in Spanish.

1847—Rochester (New York) *North Star,* Founded and edited by Frederick Douglass, it was one of the best of the numerous antislavery newspapers published during this period. The oldest Black paper in the country, *Freedom's Journal,* was founded in 1827 in New York City.

1847—Chicago (Illinois) *Daily Journal.*

1847—San Francisco (California). Two small papers were started that merged in 1849 to become *Alta California.* Bret Harte and Mark Twain were reporters for this paper. By 1853, San Francisco had a dozen dailies.

1849—St. Paul (Minnesota) *Pioneer Press.*

1850—Salt Lake City (Utah) *Deseret News,* founded and maintained to this day by the Mormon Church. "Deseret" means "land of the honey bee," according to Mormon tradition.

1850s—St. Louis (Missouri) supported six to ten papers, three of which were consolidated under Joseph Pulitzer and formed the foundation of his journalism empire.

1852—Olympia (Washington) *Columbian,* which became *Washington Pioneer,* the newspaper that announced gold discoveries and drew the "rush" north from California.

1852—Cleveland (Ohio) *Leader.*

1854—Leavenworth (Kansas) *Weekly Herald.*

1855—Omaha *Nebraskan.*

1858—Genoa (Nevada) *Territorial Enterprise,* edited by Mark Twain for a short time in the 1860s.

1859—Tubac (Arizona) *Weekly Arizonian.*

1859—Denver (Colorado) *Rocky Mountain News.* Ownership of this paper was decided by an agreed-on race between two printers. The first to get his press set up, and an issue printed, won the right to publish the only paper in town.

Frederick Douglass, powerful champion of the antislavery cause who founded the Rochester *North Star*.

According to Edward E. Cross in *The Weekly Arizonian* in 1859, "Conducting a paper in a frontier country is always a perilous, precarious and thankless task." In comparison with the dangers that menaced frontier editors, the mere jailing of James Franklin and John Peter Zenger in Colonial times was gentlemanly behavior. For example, the following item appeared in the *Marion County* (Kansas) *Record* in 1876: "Embry, who shot Anthony, editor of the *Leavenworth Times,* has been acquitted. That's just the way with some juries—they think it no more harm to shoot an editor than a Jack-rabbit."

When Sioux Falls, South Dakota, was attacked by Indians in 1862, the Indians tossed the printing press into the Big Sioux River and melted down the type to make decorative inlays for peace pipes, which they later sold to the settlers.

In the 1830s, when Texas was fighting Mexico, Gail Borden, Jr., one of the owners of the San Felipe *Telegraph and Texas Register,* lost the paper when General Santa Ana's army seized the plant and threw all the equipment into Buffalo Bayou. Borden, who created the slogan, "Remember the Alamo!," later invented a process for condensing milk and formed the dairy company that still bears his name.

James Gordon Bennett, whose *New York Herald* started so many things,

Women compositors set type for an issue of the *Quenemo* (Kansas) *Workman* in the late nineteenth century. (*Courtesy,* Kansas State Historical Society)

might also have started the California Gold Rush. A *Herald* correspondent, who was also a government official in California, sent Bennett either a sample of gold dust or a gold nugget. Some historians say one; some, the other. Although the sample lay around the office for months before anyone thought to have it evaluated, once Bennett read the assay report, he wrote about the gold in several editions in his pithy, pungent style, then published three extra editions in December, 1848, and January, 1849, entitled the *California Herald*. Historians believe that Bennett's sensationalizing of the news stimulated the famous rush. Gold also rushed into the *Herald's* bank account as people bought out all editions.

Frontier editors frequently were menacing as well as menaced. For instance, "Long John" Wentworth, editor of the Chicago *Weekly Democrat*, later U.S. Congressman and Mayor of Chicago, who earned his nickname because of the size of his feet, took an axe and a squad of officers to demolish a criminal gang's headquarters. Others were involved in equally violent escapades. William Byers, winning printer in the Denver competition, was

Give-aways and premiums for subscriptions have a long history in the publishing world. In the late nineteenth century, A. S. Bliton, publisher of the *Medford* (Oregon) *Mail*, parked his premium wagon in front of the newspaper office, displaying the bicycle, rifles, and sewing machine he was offering. (*Courtesy,* Southern Oregon Historical Society)

This sketch of the print shop of the *Rocky Mountain News*, with eight rifles and two revolvers very much in evidence, was William Byers' message to the outlaws who had kidnapped him. Byers is the dignified gentleman on the right, quill pen in hand, writing a fire-eating editorial. The clumsy contraption in the back is a manually operated flatbed press. The two men on the left are hand-setting type. (*Courtesy*, Denver Library Western History Dept.)

Schools in 'the Oklahoma Indian Territory in the 1800s were far
in advance of their time, teaching both boys and girls printing,
typesetting, and newspaper production. The students shown in
this photograph are the editorial staff of a school newspaper,
The Cherokee Rosebud, in 1848. (*Courtesy*, Oklahoma Historical
Society)

kidnapped by outlaws, but beat up a couple of them and escaped. One of
the owners of the *Weekly Arizonian* was shot while resisting arrest for stage
coach robbery.

   Although Western newspapers were as politically oriented and influential as those in the East, news from Washington and other politically important places reached them slowly. California had to rely first on ships that
took over six weeks, then on the Overland Stage that took over three weeks.
The Pony Express, founded originally for mail delivery at $5 to $10 per
letter, was also used for news dispatches. As the early colonists on the East

coast eagerly waited for each ship to bring news, so the Western settlers eagerly waited for each stage coach, each Pony Express rider, each casual traveler who was entrusted with papers. The invention of the telegraph, then the telephone, ended the days of "old" news.

The newspaper structure in the West was built upon the same foundation as that in the East—money and politics. Because journalism was supposedly more sophisticated in the 1800s than the 1700s, certain variations on the theme were played. Publishers might be supported by "contributions" from political parties to write certain stories, for example, or groups of affluent politicians might band together to hire editors to publish papers for them. Sometimes the relationship of the politicians and editors was known; more often, it was not.

Another variation appeared in the religious papers published by church groups and supported by donations from members of the congregations. These papers had considerably less impact upon the general population than did the commercial papers.

Meanwhile, back in Washington in the 1840s and 1850s, political parties lost their control of newspapers as a result of several movements. New York and other metropolitan papers, growing more powerful every year, opened Washington offices staffed by their own reporters; a Washington "agent" of the fledgling Associated Press was established; and President Lincoln severed the final tie to the "party press" when he refused to name a specific newspaper as his "party organ" at his inauguration as all his predecessors had done.

Growth of speedy news transmittal from the capital to outlying areas depended upon erecting telegraph lines. Prior to the telegraph, news gatherers relied upon boats and ponies, as we've seen. Some also used carrier pigeons. The first two were accepted by traditional use, but the telegraph companies harassed the pigeons, calling them unfair competition, and frequently capturing, shooting, or otherwise interfering with them.

The high prices that the telegraph companies charged to transmit dispatches from city to city, plus the rumor that the New York telegraph company was planning to set up a news gathering agency to sell material to papers and thereby control the flow of news, stimulated the creation of "cooperative" news gathering. Bennett and one of his competitors covered the Mexican War so effectively on a cooperative basis that, the following year, they and representatives of the six biggest and most influential New York papers—fierce competitors all—formed the original Associated Press. The AP identification appears on much that you read in the papers today, and you hear AP coverage read as part of radio and television newscasts without identification.

Although the *New York Times* is considered the inventor of the objective, nonpartisan political news report, the members of the Associated

Press more or less forced their own papers into that tradition because their newsman had to compose the same report for publication in several newspapers of different political affiliation. The AP "agent," as he was then called, was frequently in a key position because of his close identification with the use of telegraph wires. For example, on August 17, 1858, Queen Victoria's message of congratulations to President Buchanan upon completion of the Atlantic cable between the United States and England was delivered to an AP agent. He took it to President Buchanan, convinced him it was not a hoax, then took the president's handwritten reply back to the office to transmit to London. He also did a little transmitting to his member newspapers.

An AP agent also managed to transmit the news of Lincoln's assassination from Washington to New York just before all the telegraph lines were either closed down or in government use. Another "wire service" man provided the world with the news of the shooting of President Kennedy just two or three minutes after it happened. Merriman Smith of United Press-International was riding in the front seat of the presidential car in Dallas, grabbed the car telephone, and called his bureau. The flash went out to every UPI subscriber, print and electronic alike, setting off the alarm bells on hundreds of UPI teletypes throughout the world.

In the last quarter of the nineteenth century, competition among newspapers for the public's attention and business's advertising dollar was as fierce as it has been among all the media in the last twenty years. Between them, William Randolph Hearst and Joseph Pulitzer, in a circulation battle, are thought by many to have started the Spanish American War. Hearst is reputed to have wired Frederick Remington, the artist, "You provide the pictures; I'll provide the war." Ever since, reporters have been actively pursuing information, sometimes having to outsmart and overcome powerful forces to get it. The public interest was frequently the media's interest, too. Because politically, financially, militarily, and socially powerful people considered their actions no one else's business, not even the business of people who would be most affected, reporters had to break through walls of secrecy to reveal private manipulations of public monies, public votes, and public interests. To get their information, reporters frequently played the role of detectives. Getting a "scoop" and having an "exclusive" on the street before other papers also had the information meant greater status for the paper and helped it capture a larger reading public. A larger readership meant more people would see the advertising, which meant more advertisers and more revenue, which meant more power for the paper.

Once a publication had become financially and politically established, its members could begin to work for journalistic ideals. Most journalists believe in the people's right to know what is happening in their government, in the business and financial communities, and in the military. For example, the Pulitzer Prize in 1973 went to the Washington (D.C.) *Post* for its coverage of the Watergate Presidential campaign scandal. As part of a recent decision in a court case involving monopolistic practices in the media, the late Supreme Court Justice Hugo Black said that the First Amendment to the Constitution "rests on the assumption that the widest possible dissemination of information from diverse and antagonistic sources is essential to the welfare of the public."

The goal of financially secure and politically responsible newspaper publishers and editors from the late 1800s through the 1940s was complete coverage of all important events, written in accurate, nonpartisan, objective detail. Emotions were underplayed, facts emphasized, with fact and opinion separated as completely as humanly possible within the political context of each newspaper. Within this context of news reporting, publishers, editors, reporters, and photographers were convinced that newspapers could acquire community respect, and they were right. In spite of lapses from the ideal, by the time radio and television journalism arrived, newspapers had succeeded so well that the idea of the true, fair, objective news report was firmly established in people's minds as the standard for all journalism. Generations of people grew up believing and respecting the integrity of the information they read.

However, since the end of World War II, confidence in journalism has eroded because of the growth of the publicity and public relations industry, which will be discussed in Chapter 7, and also because of what has been called "reporting the human side of the news."

There is a definition for news given to all journalism students and beginning reporters. It goes like this: Dog bites man is not news. Man bites dog—that's news. In spite of this tradition, however, we are getting a majority of dog-bites-man news in all the media today in the name of "the human side of the news." It really means emphasizing the emotions of anyone involved regardless of what is really happening.

For example, City officials announce that three apartment buildings have to be torn down because they are structurally unsafe and have been for the last twenty years. The dangerous areas are listed and described. The people living in the buildings will be provided with other quarters. But news reports concentrate on the emotions of the people who have to move, giving the conditions of the building and the individual responsibilities of the landlord and the city only the briefest mention. This is the "human side of the news." The people's sorrow and dismay at having to leave their homes is only natural. It is the obvious, dog-bites-man part of the news that should be *part* of the reporting. However, current media philosophy of "reporting the human side of the news" has so emphasized, enlarged, and isolated emotional reactions that they appear to be the whole story.

During one trial for the murder of 25 people, news reports concentrated on describing and picturing the emotions of the accused man's wife and various grief-stricken relatives. At the conclusion of the trial, less space and time were devoted to the man's conviction and the evidence for it than to the emotions of one juror who had second thoughts and talked freely about her confusions. The grief and tears of the man's wife were again reported at length. What else would the poor woman do? This is emphasizing the obvious, the natural, the dog-bites-man aspect of the situation. Neither the wife's display of emotion nor the one juror's confusions had anything to do with the truth or falsity of the murder charge and actually played no part in the accused man's fate, but were so over-emphasized that people were left with the feeling that the man might have been falsely convicted. This is "reporting the human side of the news."

One more example from the dozens one can find almost daily: An airliner was struck by lightning and fell in a residential area. Residents rushed immediately to the passengers' aid and pulled as many as possible from the burning wreckage. One man, telling his story, said that, when he came out of his house, the people in the plane were yelling and screaming. "What were they saying?" a TV reporter asked. "What would you expect?" he replied in amazement. "They were yelling 'Help!' Get me out!' "

And what *would* you expect? That reporter's question was the obvious, dog-bites-man element that is over-emphasized in contemporary reporting.

Over-emphasizing emotions in daily reporting is only one step away from exploiting them. One example of extreme and tasteless exploitation of genuine sorrow was a television "memorial" two years after the death of several students at Ohio's Kent State when National Guardsmen were called in to help control a campus riot. The viewing audience was shown a half-hour of one weeping set of parents after another, who, between sobs, told what their child could have been doing had he lived. The verbal motif that rang constantly in the viewer's ears was the accusation: "Nothing has been done," directed at college officials, National Guard, state and national governments. It meant that no punishment (revenge?) had been meted out. It took very little knowledge of editing procedures to realize what point the network was making or who it was needling; however, the majority of viewers, particularly students, were so overwhelmed with emotion that it was impossible for them to think rationally, much less identify the manipulative techniques used to produce their predetermined response. Students were upset for days after that particularly tasteless example of "reporting the human side of the news." Unfortunately, it is not an isolated example.

The New Journalism, a product of the 60s, is also made up of expressions of emotions—the emotions of the journalists. The New Journalists are advocates. They take sides. Their support and their reactions are fully expressed. At its best, their brand of journalism produces moving documents; at its worst, superficial sentimentalism, maudlin attacks, and absurd symbolism. But the question still remains to be asked: Of what importance are a journalist's own emotions to the events?

What confidence can the public have in reports primarily detailing emotions in the name of news? Such reporting makes world happenings seem like one long soap opera and leaves thoughtful people wondering what really happened. What *was* the significant information? How much can we trust news reports?

Activities

1. From either the school library or local public libraries, investigate the beginnings of newspapers in your area. Discover answers to the following questions:

(1) Are the same papers in existence today? Trace changes in ownership.

(2) What is the longest time lapse between an event and the publication of the event in the oldest paper you could find?

(3) What are the physical differences, such as in kinds of type and illustrations, between the older papers and today's?

(4) What are the differences in physical placement of such elements as advertising and items of political, sports, social, and theater news between then and now?

2. Identify the local newspaper "characters." Choose one on whom to do a biographical investigation and decide, in the course of your investigations, what made him or her so colorful. If possible, find descendants or relatives to interview. Tape record their interviews and, together with photographs and quoted material from your subject's own articles, report your findings.

Alternate Assignment: Choose one of journalism's innovative historical personalities for your biographical investigation. Consider James Gordon Bennett, Horace Greeley, William Randolph Hearst, or Joseph Pulitzer among the men, or Nellie Bly (whose real name was Elizabeth Cochrane), Margaret Fuller, Jane Grey Swisshelm, or Sara Willis Parton among the women. These suggestions are very limited. Any detailed history of journalism will provide many more.

> *The chief business of the American people is business.*
>
> President Calvin Coolidge
> January , 1925, meeting of American
> Society of Newspaper Editors

> *The gargoyle's mouth is a loud-speaker, powered by the*
> *vested interest of a two-billion dollar industry, and back of*
> *that the vested interests of business as a whole, of*
> *industry, of finance. It is never silent, it drowns out all*
> *other voices, and it suffers no rebuke, for is it not the*
> *voice of America?*
>
> James Rorty
> *Our Master's Voice,* 1934

Chapter 6
Pattern-Setting in Electronic Media

Advance Preparation

1. Collect phonograph records and tapes from local libraries, private collectors, and commercial outlets to illustrate radio programming of all types, from newscasts and Presidential addresses to soap opera. Some programs easily available include Orson Welles' 1938 Mercury Theater broadcast, "War of the Worlds," a series of cuts from various types of programs assembled into albums called *Great Moments in Radio*, and a similar series of highpoints of radio newscasts, including Edward R. Murrow's World War II London broadcasts.

2. Contact the networks, television libraries of nearby colleges and universities, and commercial outlets for films of early television programs.

3. Video-tape a selection of typical contemporary television fare. Tape record a selection of typical contemporary radio fare.

4. Investigate local sources or write the networks to find out what television documentaries are now available for educational use.

5. Invite representatives, such as a Program Director, News Director, Chief Engineer, or General Manager, from local radio and television stations to describe the following aspects of their work:

(a) Trends in current programming.
(b) How network affiliation operates.
(c) Requirements of Federal Communications Commission and how they are met.
(d) Role of advertising in programming.
(e) What "ratings" are and how they work.
(f) How a news broadcast is put together.
(g) Description of station ownership.

Foundation of the Electronic Media

The original development of the electronic media was different from that of the print media in many ways; however, in the most important way it was the same. Where newspaper's beginnings are stories of individual effort and individual ownership, radio's beginnings are stories of individual effort and corporate ownership. Although the electronic media grew up independent of the print media, they were built upon the same kind of foundation, one made up of political influence and money.

Radio arrived near the end of the nineteenth century, when the nation's industrial corporate structure was developing into the "American Way of Business." Holding companies, interlocking ownerships, and monopolies that formed during the Civil War became increasingly entrenched following World War I, and it was at this time that most of the ownership of print and electronic media combined. Following World War II, when diversification became the keynote of corporate operations, many large companies diversified by buying up newspaper plants, magazine publishing companies, radio stations, and television stations. Or a combined radio-television ownership merged with newspaper ownership, and the resulting corporation acquired magazine and book publishing subsidiaries.

Today it is common for print and electronic media to be owned by one corporation and for that corporation to also own such diverse businesses as a baseball team, several factories supplying electrical equipment to government installations, thousands of acres of farming land, and a bacon packing company. Interlocking communications-industrial-governmental structures are the order of business. It is not unusual, in one town, for both morning and evening newspapers to be owned by the same corporation. This corporation may also own a radio station a hundred miles away and two television stations in another section of the state. Just accidentally the radio and television stations are affiliated with the same network, and the

newspapers' editor-in-chief is a son-in-law of the president of the corporation that owns the network. A congressman from the state in which the
newspapers, radio, and television stations are located just accidentally happens to own stock in both the corporation and network, to be on the
Congressional Committee that awards contracts for electrical equipment,
and to be an old fraternity buddy of that editor son-in-law. All coinci-
dental, of course. Such coincidences are not limited to a statewide combination of media, industry, and politics, but also occur nationwide. On a
day-to-day viewing and reading basis, it is very difficult to know who owns
what, but it is on the basis of who owns what that major editorial and
programming decisions are made.

Radio and Television History

Before radio and television, the major reason a newspaper could ask
for the advertiser's dollars and the public's nickels was its access to information that it could place on sale within hours of the event. Almost every
invention stimulated by the print medium has had behind it the push of
"immediacy," the desire to increase speed from printer to reader. Electrical communication by telegraph and telephone wire reduced even more
the time between the event and the public's knowledge of it. Radio's wireless communication introduced on-the-spot, live coverage of major events that
not only increased "immediacy," but gave the public a sense of participation in world events. Then television accidentally achieved the impossible
by broadcasting the actual historical *instant* of a momentous disaster in
1963, in Dallas, Texas, when Jack Ruby shot Lee Oswald, the suspected
assassin of President John Kennedy, before the whole nation—a nation
already emotionally torn to shreds by the President's death and funeral.

Oswald was being moved by police from one jail to another; television
cameramen were jockeying for position in the crowd to get a clear view
of him, when Ruby suddenly, unexpectedly, loomed before the cameras,
his arm outstretched. A shot sounded, Oswald dropped, chaos erupted, with
cameras swinging wildly, trying to show everyone's reaction at once, and
some kind of an ultimate had been achieved in the "immediacy quotient"
of news reporting. Whose great-grandfather, straining to hear Detroit or
Los Angeles, say, through earphones on his experimental radio in the
barn, could have imagined watching such an event?

Radio's beginnings are full of such great-grandfathers. If they weren't
straining to hear through earphones, they had learned Morse code and set
up amateur radio stations. So many great-grandfathers tinkered with radio
and radio equipment in the early days, that "firsts" took place indepen-
dently all over the country. Although radio "hams" still form a large group

today, the development of commercial radio is another story, one that is not only technically complex, but industrially and politically complex simultaneously. Time and events have only increased these initial complexities.

The beginnings of the electronic media involved, as they continue to do today, giant industrial complexes, political influence, and military concerns. From the end of the Civil War to the beginning of the 1900s, the techniques of exploitation and control of telegraph and telephone facilities that led to the formation of the giant monopoly, the American Telephone and Telegraph Company, established the business climate and provided the pattern of growth for both radio and television broadcasting. Those early years were a time of such chaos that historians of the electronic media may write several volumes trying to document events clearly and still feel dissatisfied with the results. So many events took place simultaneously; so many inventors contributed to the final product that the public bought and placed in their living rooms; so much patriotism and profiteering, good and bad politics were interwoven with commercial maneuvering and spontaneous business growth, that, by comparison, the history of print media seems simplistic.

However, out of the early confusion, the names of three men emerge Guglielmo Marconi, Lee de Forest, and David Sarnoff. The major credit for radio's original technical development goes to Marconi and de Forest, with Reginald Fessenden, Edwin Armstrong, and Ernst Alexanderson playing important, if secondary, roles. The major credit for developing broadcasting as we know it today goes to David Sarnoff of RCA whose life story is practically the life story of the broadcasting industry.

Marconi proved it possible to transmit sound waves by air; de Forest invented the radio tube by which human sound was made available to the listener; Fessenden invented the heterodyne circuit which, with the help of Alexanderson's electrical alternator, achieved long distance transmission of intelligible sound; and Armstrong invented the superheterodyne circuit which increased sensitivity of receivers so much that small, indoor, home models became possible. When all these inventions were finally put together, radio broadcasting for entertainment, for merchandise sales, for political influence and religious purposes all became possible, and the world entered America's living rooms. One of the major reasons the world entered as it did was the development of the Radio Corporation of America and the subsequent influence of David Sarnoff.

Between 1896 and 1900, Marconi patented his wireless apparatus in Britain and organized Marconi International Marine Communications with specific plans to create a world monopoly of wireless communication. In 1901, he performed the experiment that sent a radio signal across the Atlantic Ocean. Marconi, who early realized the monetary and political

Radio pioneer Guglielmo Marconi, shown with the wireless equipment he invented.

possibilities of the wireless era, was the son of a rich and politically powerful family. He, therefore, was able to start at the top and aggressively pursued his policy of world domination until the end of World War I. At that time, in America, because of patent complications, RCA loosened Marconi's control and purchased the assets of American Marconi.

Lee de Forest, the son of a minister, with a Ph.D. from Yale, starved himself in rented rooms in Chicago to buy equipment, conduct his early experiments, and form his own small company. His most important invention, in 1906, was the *audion*, the original name of radio's vacuum tube, which made intelligible sound, as different from dots and dashes, available to the casual listener. De Forest's company was in a direct competition with Marconi's worldwide organization and went bankrupt. In 1913, American Marconi acquired de Forest's United Wireless Telegraph Company and achieved monopoly of American wireless communications. However, between 1913 and 1914, American Telegraph and Telephone bought both telephone and radio rights to de Forest's audion, which led to tremendous legal complications for more than twenty years.

De Forest was a brilliant and versatile man whose inventive genius is beyond question. His lack of business sense, however, placed him in vulnerable positions. Although his inventiveness was never exhausted—he experimented with sound motion pictures, early television cameras, and did work that contributed to FM broadcasting—during the bulk of his adult life, until his death in 1961, he was financially, mentally, and emotionally drained by legal battles over patents and patent infringements.

Legal battles over patent ownership and use were practically the only constants in a rapidly developing, shifting, and changing field such as that of the early days of radio. The inventors, their corporate employers, the companies that bought rights to inventions, the people who improved upon some feature of another's invention, then patented the new feature, were all involved in bringing infringement suits or defending themselves. Many of the disputes hinged on the fact that one person's part of an invention could not work without another person's part, while still a third person might own the patent for the electrical connections that would make all the parts work together.

Large companies such as American Telephone and Telegraph, General Electric, and Marconi used these legal battles to protect and reinforce their monopolistic aims. Inventors like de Forest were squeezed out of business and forced to sell their patents for pennies. Others, like GE's Alexanderson, developed their inventions in a company's research laboratories, under contract to patent the items in the company's name. Some companies paid the inventors a share of the profits; some did not.

The Federal government stepped into the radio world as the result of the *Titanic* tragedy. Although passengers of several sinking ships had been saved when wireless calls for help reached nearby ships who raced to the rescue, the *Titanic* disaster dramatized the inadequacies of the system then in use. As a result of the government's investigation, the Radio Law of 1912 was passed. It reserved the 500-kilocycle wave length for distress calls, made increased equipment on shore and aboard ship mandatory, and enforced the interchange of messages regardless of which wireless apparatus was used. Until that law took effect, British Marconi, for example, could and did refuse to transmit messages relayed through any other company's equipment and would accept messages from the U.S. or U.S. ships only through American Marconi equipment and Marconi operators.

The Radio Act of 1912 also required government licensing of all radio stations, as well as government assignment of broadcast channels. However, Congress did not set conditions under which a license could be refused; therefore, none ever was. In addition, Congress specifically wrote into the Act that the Secretary of Commerce and Labor, who was placed in charge, could not regulate what was broadcast. Although new legislation applying to the broadcast industry has been created and amended, then amended again, this basic prohibition still stands. At the time of the Radio Act of 1912, use of radio broadcasting was for private interchange of business messages, not for general broadcasts to the public. When commercial broadcasting developed, the Act proved inadequate. A new Act was passed in 1927; however, by that time the pattern of contemporary commercial broadcasting had already been set. The years between the end of World War I and the passage of the Radio Act of 1927 established the patterns of broadcasting and the essential practices by which the industry operates today.

During World War I, the U.S. Navy was given control of all radio communications. These were used primarily for messages sent ship-to-shore and ship-to-ship. At the end of the shooting war, the commercial-legal-political war started again, with major battles taking place in Congress and New York offices between the leading electrical equipment manufacturers and the Federal government, with the small, independent companies buffeted about by the wrestling giants. This war was a war for control —control of patents, control of station licenses, control of what later became advertising and programming—in fact, control of everything concerning the "public" air waves.

While the battle took place in Congress in 1918 and 1919 to decide whether or not radio should be government owned, as in Europe, or released by the Navy to competitive commercial development, private organizations that subsequently took over the industry were being formed.

The Navy actually held the radio properties until 1920, but on October 17, 1919, the Radio Corporation of America was formed by three major industrial concerns—Westinghouse, General Electric, and American Telephone & Telegraph Company. The plans were for RCA to sell the radio equipment and hold patents on other equipment for the exclusive use of the three companies, a procedure called "cross-licensing" that was designed to break legal stalemates about patent infringements. Westinghouse and GE would earn extra money by manufacturing home radio receivers and AT&T would manufacture and sell transmitting equipment. All three would operate transmitters; that is, radio stations. Shortly after these original agreements were made, United Fruit Corporation became one of the partners because it held patents on pieces of radio equipment that could not otherwise have been used because of legal entanglements.

Although the Radio Corporation of America was formed partly to break down the obstacles then preventing commercial manufacture and sale of wireless broadcasting equipment, another goal of the manufacturers who formed the company was to create a commercial monopoly. Owen D. Young, the attorney for General Electric who invented the idea of RCA, did not foresee public broadcasting as we know it now, nor did the executives of the other corporations. They saw two things—a further extension of their manufacturing monopolies of electrical equipment and a further extension of the use of telephones. However, David Sarnoff, the man chosen to manage RCA, was one who, like many others scattered throughout the country, saw the entertainment possibilities of radio.

David Sarnoff, like Andrew Carnegie and Joseph Pulitzer, is an example of the penniless, self-taught, industrious immigrant boy who rose to wealth and power. He taught himself the Morse code as a teenager, started with American Marconi as an errand boy, became a telegraph operator, and happened to be the one on duty in New York in 1912 to keep in touch with the sinking *Titanic*. It was literally through the hand of this twenty-one year old telegrapher that the United States learned of the disaster and that, finally, the *Carpathia* managed to pick up as many survivors as its crew could find in the ocean. While Sarnoff was trying to

Young David Sarnoff in 1908, age 17, at the start of his long career. At 16, Sarnoff taught himself Morse Code, got a job as errand boy in Marconi's New York shop, was promoted to wireless operator at Nantucket Island's Siasconset Station (shown here), later was transferred to a New York City station where he was on duty in 1912 when the *Titanic* sank. (Wide World Photos)

reach the *Carpathia*, President Taft ordered every other radio station off the air. The whole country, from President to street cleaner, waited breathlessly, in agony, to learn which name David Sarnoff would write next as the reports of the living and dead slowly, faintly, clicked in from the *Carpathia*'s wireless operator. Sarnoff stayed at his post for seventy-two hours, keeping in communication with the *Carpathia* as she neared New York, until the lists were complete. David Sarnoff was by then a national celebrity, as important as any one of his own television celebrities in later years, and from then on, he was in a key position both to develop and control electronic media.

When investigation showed that the loss of life in the *Titanic* disaster could have been cut down by at least two-thirds had there been better wireless equipment and operators on duty twenty-four hours, the radio equipment business boomed. American Marconi and Sarnoff boomed with it.

In 1916, three years before RCA was formed, Sarnoff suggested to American Marconi that they put on the market what he called a "Radio Music Box" for home use to receive concerts and lectures. Although Marconi wasn't interested, and later RCA executives were only lukewarm to the idea, by the early 1920s, when radio broadcasts by amateur station owners, similar to the ones Sarnoff had in mind, leaped into popularity throughout the country, Sarnoff and RCA went into action. In the following years, when government antitrust action forced the break-up of the companies involved in RCA, Sarnoff became head of RCA and created NBC and its original two networks. In 1969, when he retired from RCA as Chairman of its Board of Directors, he had influenced the direction of both radio and television broadcasting more than any other single person. He died in 1971, aged 80.

Programming Patterns Set

The years immediately after World War I, during which big business and government maneuvered for control of the emerging broadcast industry, were an energetic, although short-lived, period of enthusiastic development of radio by thousands of amateurs. Across the nation, these people broadcast from their back bedroom, a corner of a barn, the attic, or a small shack on the north forty, mainly for the fun of it. A number of them accidentally stumbled into broadcasting directly to the public for the benefit of sponsors. During their transmission periods, broadcasters grew tired of talking into the microphones and began playing their own phonograph records. In each area, from some back bedroom in Hollywood, to that garage near Pittsburgh that housed equipment later to become KDKA, some enterprising mer-

This barn was the site of the first broadcast, in 1921, of the radio station which became KMED, the Voice of Southern Oregon. Started for fun by William J. Virgin and some of his friends, the station has become a large, profitable, and influential organization. (*Courtesy*, KMED Radio and TV)

chant offered the broadcaster an unlimited supply of phonograph records in return for announcing the name of the shop supplying them.

For radio, the early 1920s corresponds in vitality, enthusiasm, and experimentation to the early 1830s for newspapers. Anyone with a little know-how, a little money, and a great deal of enthusiasm could get into broadcasting. Private individuals, educational institutions, small businesses and large corporations enthusiastically started radio stations for various reasons and multiplied by hundreds across the country. Individuals started stations for the fun of it at first and later, for money; educational institutions, to extend their activities beyond campus boundaries; businesses, both small and large, to stimulate sales by creating good will and keeping their names before the public.

Some stations changed their amateur status for the beginnings of commercial status when individual owners took the equipment out of the living room, attic, back bedroom, barn, or garage, and made it part of a business. First, the transmitter and all its clumsy parts were squeezed into a closet, a corner of a storeroom, an improvised shack on the roof, or some other out-of-the-way place; then anyone who had shown interest in radio, from vice president to errand boy, was put in charge, or the owner himself operated the transmitter for a few hours a week. As this adult toy grew in commercial importance, individual commercial enterprises were founded with space and staff of their own, many of which became important stations that brought their early enthusiast-owners great financial and political returns. Others, including most educational radio stations, died quietly of malnutrition, were bought up, or killed off by either local commercial stations or the networks, as the sections on network growth and government regulations will show.

The thousands of original broadcasters ranged from salesmen to engineers, from newspaper owners to college professors, who enthusiastically did-it-themselves, constructing transmitters either by building the parts and putting them together or by putting together parts manufactured by companies involved in patent infringement litigations. These companies could not put the parts together themselves to sell a whole transmitter, and AT&T refused to sell whole transmitters in order to keep control of the market, but the public was not bound by the GE–AT&T–Westinghouse agreements. The public did not know, and probably wouldn't have cared had they known, of the purpose of RCA's patent pool. However, the actions of these early radio broadcasters, happily experimenting in an area the three corporations had marked out for their own and successfully broadcasting before these corporations could get their stations and networks firmly established, had deep and permanent effects on broadcasting.

The spontaneous growth of broadcasting and its eventual confinement to the pattern that we know today, the solidifying of early program experimentation into the mold we have grown up with, and the extension of advertising throughout broadcasting to shift expenses of stations from owners to sponsors, all took place simultaneously within the same short ten years, approximately 1920–30. By the Golden Age of Radio, the '30s and '40s, the patterns were all set. Television took them over while radio limited itself to aspects of the original pattern that were still workable in terms of its reduced status.

The spontaneous growth of radio stations, established primarily as hobbies or experiments, took place mainly between 1919 and 1921. The following short list of very early ones is given to show the variety of stations that sparked the beginning of the electronic media:

9XM, University of Wisconsin, later WHA, Madison.
8MK, later WWJ, Detroit, started by owner of Detroit *News*.
6ADZ, later KNX, Hollywood, California.
4XD, later WBT, Charlotte, North Carolina.
9CT, later WDAP, Chicago, Illinois.
9ZJ, later WLK, Indianapolis, Indiana.
8XK, later KDKA, Pittsburgh, Pennsylvania.
8ZA, later KFGZ, Emmanuel College, Berrien Springs, Michigan.
9FD, Purdue College, Lafayette, Indiana.

At first, the novelty of the equipment was all important. The *magic* of human voices coming out of the air created both fear and fascination. As with every new fad, radio was both denounced and praised. It was either credited as the source of every good, from sunny weather to improved education and the general increase of culture—but more often as the

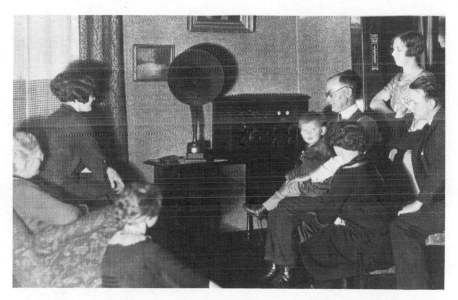

This photograph of the A. D. Birch family of Topeka, Kansas, was taken in 1922, not to record the three generations of the family, but to show their prize possession—the radio—complete with a dozen dials and the horn for amplification. Although this picture is obviously posed, it is nonetheless a true representation of family listening that lasted through World War II. (*Courtesy*, Kansas State Historical Society)

great source of increased business—or damned as the root of every evil, from crop failure to short hair and the advent of cigarettes—but more often as the great source of increased immorality. After all, the Establishment was still trying to accept the horseless carriage, young men without beards, young ladies with short hair—after World War I, *cutting* hair was an act of youthful rebellion—cut-down shoes for men, short skirts for women—after World War II, long skirts came back—with more horrors to come. After cutting their hair, young women didn't burn their bras; they just threw those restraints away, along with their corsets and many social taboos.

Young men, refusing to wear long sideburns, beards, boots, or tight trousers, even refused to go into their father's business or profession. Those who did had to face their father's resistance when they tried to reorganize the business according to "modern" ideas. The post-World War I period was an era of upheaval as radical, with as large a generation gap, as the 1960s. New lifestyles were forged, and during the disruptive and painful process, the Establishment held its collective heads in anger and despair, hating what might come next. Radio? Just one "damned" thing after another, using "damned" in its religious sense.

Even after being "damned" by countless "right-thinking, God-fearing, clean-cut, 100-percent patriotic American citizens," radio did not disappear in a spurt of hellfire, and eventually, fascination and profit won out over fear. In 1920, 600 stations broadcast an hour or two a day; by the end of 1922, stations were operating in every state, with the East and West coast states claiming the largest numbers; by 1924, 1400 were on the air for several consecutive hours daily; by 1927 continuous broadcasting from 6 A.M. to midnight was established not only as a "tradition," but also as a broadcaster's right.

Starting about 1927, a career as a "radio personality" of any kind was the newest, most exciting, and on-the-way-to-being the most profitable in the country. Every aspect of broadcasting became profitable during the 1930s. Radio was the only industry upon which the Great Depression had no effect. Radio entertainment was said to be the major unifying and comforting force in the country during the years when poverty and all its attending travail wore down the people's spirit.

From almost its very beginnings, broadcasting offered the whole spectrum of entertainment and information in programming. Entertainment programs, by individual singers and musicians, first consisted almost entirely of classical music, then shifted to popular, with emphasis on dance bands. Comedy shows, serious drama, talk shows, children's programs, and the afternoon soap operas all started in the late 1920s. Information programs from 1921 provided news, weather, sports events and scores, crop reports, stock market quotations, commentary by distinguished people on important

This serious-looking gentleman spoke to the early radio receivers of
the 1920s through a microphone known as a "tomato can." Hung
on a large hook inserted in a lamp pole, it was the smallest microphone of its era. (*Courtesy*, NBC)

issues, cooking schools with the recipes read v-e-r-y slowly, and time signals: "At the sound of the gong, it will be . . ." Sunday morning church
services were also broadcast as early as 1921.

Excepting the artists on phonograph records, which were played by
the thousands, all radio performers during the first few years were
amateurs. Singers, musicians, lecturers, elocutionists who read or recited
poetry and dramatic monologues, and politicians, elected or campaigning,
all did their thing on the air. They did their thing, that is, if they could
be coaxed to the microphone. The coaxing had to be very persuasive, be-

The radio "studio" of WBZ, Springfield, Mass., when the station started broadcasting in September, 1921. It was owned by Westinghouse. Two amateurs are performing, with the one station employee, the engineer-announcer, in the background. Note the bare walls, clutter of ponderous equipment, exposed pipes, and for some reason or other, a pencil sharpener, attached to the molding of the mantlepiece of a left-over fireplace. (Wide World Photos)

cause people frequently refused, even though the radio station offered to pay their trolley fare.

This national shyness wore off very quickly, however, and soon local stations witnessed the phenomenon of hundreds of people standing in line, waiting for an opportunity to perform over the air for nothing. The stations provided the opportunity with gratitude because filling the air with some kind of sound nonstop for several hours not only drained their inventiveness, but wore out their tonsils. The novelty of hearing sound for its own sake had dulled, and stations began putting together some kind of a program. Inventors like de Forest and Fessenden more or less set precedents by broadcasting live music. In an early experiment, Fessenden himself played violin selections and a woman friend sang. Therefore, the way to fill the air was to sing or play an instrument. Hopefully, the two or three early employees could do both, and they did to exhaustion.

Imagine how you would feel if you had to sing, play the piano, announce your own numbers, and provide a little casual talk for two or three hours without a break. Imagine also the relief you would feel when, one morning, after you had run out of friends and relations who could be coaxed to perform, you went downtown and found dozens of people asking to be put on the air. You probably would have done what the early broadcasters did—put them on, no questions asked, no auditions requested, retaining only a finger on a button to cut "radicals" off the air. A radical was anyone who spoke on subjects considered taboo at the time, like prostitution, birth control, venereal disease, cancer, and communism.

Somehow, during these early years, the fifteen-minute broadcast interval became standard. The original motivation was probably those tired

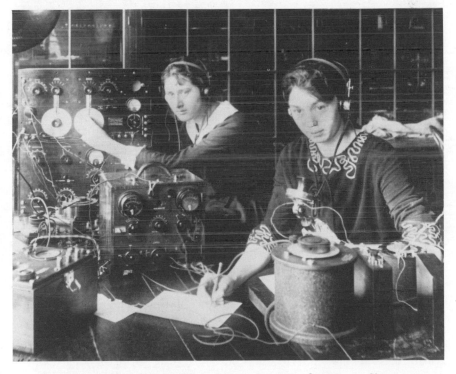

Students at Radcliffe College, Massachusetts, plug in on Chicago from newly established radio station in the 1920s. The sounds of outrage must have crackled louder than the static around the heads of these earnest young Cliffies when their relatives voiced their reaction. (Bettmann Archive)

A typical radio broadcast from a typical studio in the 1920s. At right, a phonograph for record playing when no live performer was available. The man singing into the large size tomato can microphone originally came to the studio to sing without payment, later became part of the staff because he also could speak well, play the piano, crank the phonograph, tack the soundproofing material back on the wall when it started to come down, and had lots of friends who were also voice students. The man at the piano alternated with the man singing. (*Courtesy*, NBC)

tonsils and raw throat. Then a kind of format for each fifteen-minute segment evolved, consisting of singer, instrument, singer, talk, station break, time signal, "courtesy" announcement for the station owner. If the owner was a newspaper, the listener's attention was called to the paper; if a department store, to its location; if a manufacturing company, just announcing the name was considered sufficient advertising at that time. Then the procession of entertainers began again. If someone didn't appear, the staff filled in, singing and talking until the next station break.

By the mid-1920s, professional entertainers began to make radio appearances in the large cities. At first, they too performed without pay, sometimes for the fun of the experience, sometimes as a favor to a friend, sometimes for publicity. Letters from people who heard them hundreds of miles away became a kind of remuneration until money took its place. Musicians led the demand for payment for appearances, starting in 1925.

The two or three people employed by a station owner were usually either announcers or engineers, and many an announcer developed from one of the volunteer vocalists. As radio programming developed, announcers frequently considered themselves to be "radio personalities," part actor, part comedian, and many received as much fan mail as actors and comedians.

Originally both men and women were announcers, but in 1926 women were taken off the air in that capacity. Nor did they appear as news reporters. Women could broadcast as actresses, singers, musicians, demonstrators of cooking school programs, or in any interchange with an announcer that offered "household hints." The few women politicians then in public life spoke on the air occasionally, but in general male voices dominated. It wasn't until the early 1970s that women again were heard as announcers, usually on small FM radio stations; however, at that time, they also became part of newscasts, presenting both straight news reports and feature articles, jobs they had been doing in the print media for almost a century.

Broadcast journalism first went on the air in 1922 disguised as "current events talks." Although staff announcers on the many radio stations owned by newspapers read news items regularly on the air, they read mostly headlines which were used as teasers to stimulate newspaper sales. The "current events talks," however, blended both news reports and editorial opinion for fifteen minutes in the kind of analysis-and-prediction commentary that was to become the routine of dozens of "news commentators" during the Golden Age of Radio, particularly during World War II.

The first man to make this kind of broadcast was H. V. Kaltenborn, who, in over 40 years of almost continuous broadcasting, earned the title of Dean of American Commentators. In 1922, Kaltenborn was associate editor of the Brooklyn (N.Y.) *Eagle* and a popular lecturer on current events. Until the depression ruined it, the *Eagle* was a well-known, influential daily newspaper, and Kaltenborn joined its staff in 1903 as a reporter, fresh from a year in Europe. He reached Europe by hitchhiking to New York from his home in Milwaukee—he was about 19—then traveling by cattle boat to France. He saw the Paris Exposition and toured Europe on a bicycle, selling stereoscopes and learning French. He already knew German. His father was Baron Rudolph von Kaltenborn, a Hessian Army officer who emigrated to America and married a Milwaukee school teacher.

After three years on the *Eagle,* Kaltenborn decided to attend college, enrolled at Harvard, and in 1909, graduated with honors, a Phi Beta Kappa key, and prizes in debating and elocution. He spent the next year as an Exchange Professor from Harvard to Berlin University. During this year, he met and married Baroness Olga von Nordenflycht. When they returned to America in 1910, he rejoined the *Eagle,* remaining until 1930, when the paper was hit by the depression. He then joined CBS, and in 1940 went to NBC where he remained until the end of his career.

In addition to writing prolifically for his own paper and selling articles to magazines, Kaltenborn also lectured—activities that he never abandoned when he added broadcasting to his lexicon. Kaltenborn's radio career developed from lectures on current events that he gave Tuesday mornings in the *Eagle* auditorium. In 1917, he also started to run annual *Eagle* travel tours—sometimes in the United States, sometimes abroad. These were not ordinary tours. Prime ministers, governors, mayors, town dignitaries, and celebrities met and entertained the groups. This gave Kaltenborn tremendous prestige, enormous political background, and access to important people throughout the world.

When Station WEAF decided to add "current events" to its programming, the management offered the *Eagle* the same reciprocal deal that sellers of phonograph records were offering radio stations. WEAF would provide air time and "courtesy" announcements to stimulate sale of the *Eagle* if the newspaper would provide the speaker. Kaltenborn was the obvious choice as the person most experienced in giving this kind of talk, and his commentaries set the pattern for years to come, influencing such popular commentators as Lowell Thomas, Boake Carter, Gabriel Heater, and all the other legendary voices of radio.

Kaltenborn was also the first man to bring the explosions of a real battle in a genuine war into American living rooms when he broadcast an on-the-spot report of the fight for a Spanish town in 1936, early in the Spanish Civil War. This was three years before Edward R. Murrow's famous broadcasts during the London "blitz" in World War II.

When the Spanish Civil War started, Kaltenborn was in Europe. He hurried immediately to the French-Spanish border and found that, by a freak of both geography and border treaties, a spit of French land, jutting in a sharp curve of a river, reached into the battle. Deciding to broadcast an eye witness description with genuine sound effects, Kaltenborn found an engineer to handle the mechanics, got the lines set, climbed into a haystack, called his network, and offered the report. The result was a fifteen minute broadcast in which he described burning railroad cars, maneuvers of a small armored train, shell explosions, and burning buildings to appropriate accompaniment. Although these conditions sound very mild several wars and rocket weaponry later, Kaltenborn was in great danger in that haystack.

Neither side knew he was there, bullets twice cut his cables, and safety lay a hundred yards behind him, across a bullet-swept field.

On another occasion, during the 1937 Munich Crisis that delayed World War II in Europe for two more years, Kaltenborn surpassed David Sarnoff's 1912 exploit at the Marconi telegraph key. During the 18 days that the Crisis lasted, while Prime Minister Chamberlain of England and Hitler conferred in Munich, H. V. Kaltenborn made 85 broadcasts, keeping American listeners up to date on events, analyzing and commenting upon their possible implications.

When Kaltenborn died in 1965, aged 87, he had been broadcasting and analyzing the news since 1922 with few breaks, none of them long. Although not the greatest star in radio's heaven, Kaltenborn was a trail blazer and left broadcast journalism a legacy of innovation, industry, courage, and honor from which it still draws dividends.

A few of the documented early radio programs include the following:

1920: Phonograph music broadcast over 8MK, Detroit, from the offices of the Detroit *News*, for dances.

1920: Broadcast of results of the Harding-Cox presidential election over 8MK, Detroit; KDKA, Pittsburgh; the forerunner of a San Francisco station; and 6ADZ, Hollywood, California.

1921: KDKA, Pittsburgh, the Westinghouse station, broadcast the following:

January 2: Sunday morning church services.

February 18: Talks by Alice M. Robertson, Representative from
   Oklahoma, first woman to be elected to Congress, and Col.
   Theodore Roosevelt, Jr.

April 11: Boxing match between Johnny Ray and Johnny
   Dundee.

August 4–6: Davis Cup tennis matches.

August 5: Baseball game.

1921: The RCA station, WJZ, Newark, New Jersey, broadcast the July 2 fight between U.S. Heavyweight Champion Jack Dempsey and French Champion George Carpentier, and the October World Series games were relayed by telephone, play by play, from the field to the microphone.

1922: KYW, Chicago, another Westinghouse station, started its career by devoting its broadcast time to the full performances of the Chicago Civic Opera from October 1 until the opera season concluded several months later.

1922: February 22, GE-owned WGY, Schenectady, New York, started a regular program schedule, including performances of serious drama by a group called the WGY Players.

1924: Both Republican and Democratic National Conventions broadcast.

1925: Presidential Inauguration broadcast.

1927: President Coolidge's address to a joint session of Congress broadcast. By this time regular programming was well established throughout the nation, and the networks were in their infancy.

By 1927, well-established radio stations with regular program schedules were owned by such newspapers as the Atlanta *Journal*, Kansas City *Star*, Dallas *News*, Chicago *Tribune*, Detroit *Free Press*, Miami *News*, and many others across the country. Department stores such as L. Bamberger & Company, Newark, N.J.; Gimbel Brothers, New York and Philadelphia; Strawbridge & Clothier and John Wanamaker's, both Philadelphia; and the Shepherd Stores, Boston, among others, owned and operated individual radio stations.

The beginnings of the networks line up as follows: Westinghouse-owned stations included WBZ, Springfield, Mass.; WJZ, New York; KYW, Chicago, as well as KDKA, Pittsburgh—all on the air by the end of 1921. GE-owned stations included KOA, Denver; KGO, Oakland, Calif., both started in 1924; as well as home-base WGY, Schenectady, on the air in 1922. WDY, originally in New Jersey, but moved into New York City within a year, was RCA's original station until the organization became independent and began to buy up others, including those of AT&T. As early as 1922, AT&T, originating from WEAF, New York, via a combination of telephone lines and wireless radio, sent messages from a ship off the New Jersey coast across the continent to Catalina Island, off the West coast near Los Angeles, thus proving the possibility of network operation.

While radio stations owned by large corporations, with experimental programming backed by large supplies of corporate money and access to the beginnings of the networks, were able to mount broadcasts of major events, small stations owned by individuals, educational institutions, and small businesses limped along with the amateurs. During this same period of time, advertising took over financial support of radio from the station owners in the same way it took over support of the newspapers from their original owners' printing businesses. The major difference in this progression, however, is that in print media, both newspapers and magazines, news came first, then advertising, then entertainment. In the electronic media, entertainment came first, then advertising, then news.

Advertising Moves into Radio

Although Lee de Forest broadcast product commercials in 1916 for his own equipment from his station in New York, broadcast histories usually credit transmission of the first commercials to KDKA, the Westinghouse station in Pittsburgh, in 1920, and WEAF, AT&T's station in New

York, in 1922. The first development happened in the same accidental way that marked other developments in radio at that time all over the country; the second, by deliberate sale of time to make money, according to AT&T's master plan for radio.

Dr. Frank Conrad, an engineer who worked for Westinghouse, was an enthusiastic amateur broadcaster before World War I, using his garage in Wilkinson, a suburb of Pittsburgh, to house his experimental station, 8XK. He was one of the people who tired of talking and substituted phonograph records. When he had exhausted his personal supply, he broadcast that fact and the owner of Wilkinson's Hamilton Music Store offered recordings.

Westinghouse turned 8XK into KDKA for their own commercial purposes as the result of the next series of incidents. Dr. Conrad's 8XK, which had been moved into a Westinghouse factory to test equipment during WWI, was back on the air by 1920, broadcasting music, sports results, and chitchat on a more or less regular schedule for other amateurs. Horne's Department Store in Pittsburgh, watching interest grow in radio, set up a demonstration receiver to pick up Conrad's broadcasts and advertised similar receivers for sale. A Westinghouse executive saw the possibilities immediately and got KDKA organized and on the air in time to start formal broadcasting with the Harding-Cox presidential election returns. Although other small stations, particularly Detroit's 8MK, later WWJ, owned by William E. Scripps, an amateur broadcaster and publisher of the Detroit *News*, did the same thing, none has received the acclaim, publicity, or place in history that has gone to KDKA.

Because Westinghouse owned and operated KDKA to advertise its own products, WEAF, the AT&T station in New York, gets the credit for the first sale of time for advertising purposes to an outside organization. The story goes that AT&T planned to run its radio operations in the same manner that it ran its telephone operations— as "toll" services over long distances. Lee de Forest's audion, applied to the telephone, made long distance conversation practical, and private long distance telephone conversations were priced at so much per minute. Now that radio was entering the business world, it could be offered to commerce in the same way—so much per minute of broadcasting "for the public benefit," that is, to sell products. AT&T therefore established WEAF on this master plan.

At this point in WEAF's history, stories differ. One is that many manufacturers and others with items to sell had contracted to broadcast messages to the public even before WEAF started operation, with the implication that WEAF was financially successful the moment it went on the air. Another is that AT&T poured large sums into the station, but that, of the three transmitters permitted under the original RCA cross-licensing agreements, WEAF was the only station losing money. Therefore, on August 28, 1922, the station manager sold ten minutes of time for $50 to the Queensboro Corporation to sell houses in a suburban development. However the station came to do it, broadcasting this particular commercial introduced to the public the now familiar sponsor with an advertising message.

To hear that commercial today, no one would recognize it as "a message from our sponsor." At that time, manufacturers like Westinghouse, newspapers like the Detroit *News*, retailers like Gimbel Brothers Department Stores, who used their radio stations to advertise their products, did not do so directly. An outright sales message naming products, citing advantages, downgrading "the other leading brand," or mentioning price was considered "unseemly," that is, socially vulgar, undignified, too personal, and generally offensive. The announcer in Detroit, for example, read snippets of news and weather reports between the efforts of local talent, concluding each news item with the dignified announcement, "Details can be found in the latest edition of the Detroit *News*."

Other very early commercials, like that of the Queensboro Corporation on WEAF, were incorporated into "informative talks." This particular talk was announced as one about Nathaniel Hawthorne, the novelist, and what were purported to be his ideals about community spirit and home life. The Queensboro Corporation executive who read the talk started by saying that the real estate developer honored Hawthorne's memory by naming the tract "Hawthorne Court," then spent the rest of the time plugging suburban life over city life, this particular suburb over all others.

Other examples of such "informative talks" included those that discussed cleanliness vs. beards sponsored by a razor blade company; teeth and their care by a toothpaste company; a history of greeting cards by greeting cards manufacturers; and a history of automobiles by an automobile manufacturer.

Even though business increased because of these heavily veiled commercials, advertisers noticed that informative talks did not attract the public in the numbers that music did, particularly dance music. Therefore, advertising agencies sought some way to sponsor music while staying within the limits of conservative respectability. An advertising salesman hit on the idea of naming a dance orchestra for the sponsoring company. The result was the "Browning King Orchestra," sponsored by Browning, King & Company, a firm that sold men's clothing. Advertisers immediately adopted the idea, and the "vulgarity" of advertising was cloaked, although the cloak was sometimes made of invisible material, as when the Magnolia Petroleum Company Band hit the air.

The more sophisticated of these combined advertising-broadcasting efforts originated in advertising agencies in New York and Chicago for advertisers who bought time on what later became major network stations.

These companies had long used print media and knew the value of advertising. With big money supporting this kind of advertising, many of the programs became so popular that they lasted through the Golden Age of Radio; some, into television. The most notable example of the latter was the Lucky Strike (cigarette) Orchestra and the Lucky Strike Singers on the "Lucky Strike Hit Parade." A few of the others include the Rheingold (beer) Quartet, the Seiberling (rubber company) Singers, the Goodrich Silvertown (tires) Orchestra, the A&P (grocery stores) Gypsies, and the Ipana (toothpaste) Troubadours.

The idea behind using a product name in such a socially irreproachable manner was to label the whole program with the sponsor's name. One of its great advantages was that the program could contain anything from drama to variety acts. The Eveready (batteries) Hour was one of the first to experiment with such a format, changing the content at will. A few of the others were the Kraft (cheese) Music Hall, General Motors Family Party, the Palmolive (soap) Hour, and the Philco (radio) Hour. Comedian Jack Benny customarily greeted his Sunday night audience with "Jello again . . . ," and comedian Ed Wynn's title, Texaco Fire Chief, stemmed from another such indirect advertising device. As means of popular identification, these naming devices lasted even after advertising and commercials that deliberately sold specific products had become socially acceptable.

In the early 1920s, advertising was limited by broadcasters to a few daytime hours; by 1925, as revenue mounted, advertising was extended to all daytime broadcasting hours, with assurances made frequently that night broadcasting "would never sink so low as to permit the crass commercialism of advertising." The pressure of increasing profits and insistence of both radio station employees and advertisers pushed advertising, little by little, into night-time broadcasting as well. By 1930, commercially sponsored entertainment and news broadcasts were firmly entrenched at all hours.

At first, the public objected loudly to advertising on the air for several reasons. In addition to "the vulgarity of this invasion of the homes of respectable people who wish to receive entertainment and enlightenment via the public air waves," the strongest objection, voiced in Congress, state legislatures, and other important places of public discussion, was a fear that has since come true. That fear was that a program's ability to sell products would become its only measurement. Advertisers would note only two results: (1) the number of people listening as reported by "ratings" —a system of counting listeners that, started in 1925–27, remains the deciding factor of today's commercial broadcasting—and (2) the increase of sales. All other purposes, such as education, free examination of issues, honest discussion of controversial subjects, quality of performance, aesthetic values, concern for a balance between majority and minority interests, de-

gree of public importance, would become subservient to the number of
sales and amount of money made once financial support of broadcasting
was firmly in advertisers' hands.

And so they did. They remain so today, with the rare exception of
events as politically-oriented and prestigious as the national conventions of
political parties in presidential election years or events so politically-
oriented and scandalous as the 1973 "Watergate" congressional hearings.
On these occasions, the networks point with pride at the amount of advertising money supposedly lost "in the public interest." But when an
organization's *profits*—not income, profits—continue annually to be counted
in the millions, what actually has been lost? And what political gains have
been made? To answer both questions at once: practically nothing and a
great many.

Back in the pattern-setting days between 1920 and 1930, broadcasters
simply ignored public protests against advertising until the protests stopped.
Well into the 1930s broadcast executives and government officials would
make public statements against the use of advertising on the air, while
individual radio stations and networks sold more and more time to advertising as a matter of policy. The government exerted no control even
at a time, in the mid-1920s, as we shall see, when control and protection
were desperately needed. In fact, President Coolidge's most widely quoted
remark, "The chief business of the American people is business," loosened
all restraints by 1927. At the time of The Radio Act of 1927, which is the
basis of the Communications Act of 1934, all possibility of valid, equitable,
and protective government regulation of broadcasting had long since
vanished.

Networks and Government

Let's look back again to the beginnings of broadcasting and unravel
two more of the interwoven strands of the pattern-setting years of the
electronic media—the growth of the networks and the fate of government
regulation.

These two strands are more tightly woven together than any of the
others. Had there not been close political ties between the people who desired control of broadcasting and people in the government, the situation
in today's electronic media might be different. However, such relationships
existed, the political and economic climate promoted them, and the individuals involved were sufficiently rewarded to make their actions or in-
actions worthwhile. All this together produced the pattern of network-
controlled, commercially-oriented radio broadcasting, with public service
subordinate to sales. When television arrived, it was structured to fit into
the mold already established.

The irony in the situation is that the circumstances that produced network-controlled commercial broadcasting and ineffective governmental regulation had little to do with broadcasting. The mold was primarily shaped by conflicts within the group involved in the cross-licensing agreements—AT&T–GE–Westinghouse, and their subsidiary, RCA—and what almost can be called the mechanics of government. On one side, the political side of the government, members of Congress and Cabinet members such as the Secretary of Commerce, all of whom were oriented to helping industry so that industry could help them, opposed the legal side of the government, The Federal Trade Commission and the Justice Department, who attempted to apply antitrust and antimonopolistic laws. By 1930, it was all over but the counting of money by the networks. A comment that is current in the electronic media is that a license to broadcast is "a license to print money." Here's how it happened.

Remember the sinking of the *Titanic* in 1912? Remember how the investigators' recommendations for more radio equipment and twenty-four hour duty for operators caused the wireless business to boom? Another result was a bill before Congress to give the Federal government some control of "radio telegraphy" to make sure such a disaster would not happen again. In 1912, you will recall, voice transmission was in its infancy and broadcasting as we know it was imagined only by a few individuals, one of whom was David Sarnoff at American Marconi. Interest was concentrated on sending messages by Morse code.

Although the shock of the *Titanic* disaster was deep and long-lasting, chances are that Congress might have moved much slower if the Navy had not started pushing for Federal controls. A few irresponsible practical jokers among the hundreds of enthusiastic radio "hams" were driving maritime officials crazy. These people were not only interfering with official communications, but were sending out false orders, supposedly from Admirals and other high ranking officers, that moved Naval and Coast Guard vessels around the ocean for the fun of it. Wireless messages came out of the air. Signatures could not be verified, and because there was no registration or licensing of amateurs, senders of these messages could not be identified.

Playful shifting of ships might be expensive, irritating, and potentially dangerous in a case of emergency, but even worse were the false SOS signals that sent Coast Guard, Navy, and merchant vessels on frantic midnight searches for sinking ships. The Radio Act of 1912 put an end to such antics, made transoceanic travel as safe as radio telegraphy could make it, but unfortunately, it was not designed to carry out an orderly, equitable development of a commercial broadcast industry, although it was the law under which the industry developed.

The Radio Act of 1912 was limited both in its requirements and in its legal power. It set up the following regulations: (1) Licensing of radio operators, with fines established for employment of unlicensed operators. (2) Division of radio wave lengths according to purpose. One band was reserved for distress signals; another, for all amateur transmitters; and a third, for official messages. And (3) Prohibition of interference with official radio communication and punishment for sending false signals; the punishment included both fine and imprisonment. The first two provisions were the ones applied to broadcasting directly to the public after World War I.

The narrow official expectancies for radio were clear when Congress gave the responsibility for administering the Radio Act to the Department of Commerce. You will recall the plans for world-wide domination of radio telegraphy that Marconi had going at the time, and that American Marconi was threatening AT&T, whose executives were turning their attention to the uses of wireless telephony and telegraphy. Remember also that both General Electric and Westinghouse, the largest U.S. manufacturers of electrical equipment, were beginning to realize that making wireless equipment would probably be profitable for them. All these factors set the stage for later developments.

Herbert Hoover was Secretary of Commerce during the whole period of commercial development of broadcasting, and he was in a strange position. On one hand, he was one of the people in government who were most sympathetic to the aims of the industrialists who wished to make broadcasting all their own. On the other hand, his department had to administer the one law that was supposed to handle the developing industry. Although most of his applications of the law, and some of his improvisations upon it, seemed to favor the few powerful stations owned by his friendly industrialists, nonetheless, he tried to provide a little order when air traffic became chaotic. But the Attorney General then ruled that he was exceeding his powers. The ruling permitted unlimited freedom to commercial broadcasting; therefore, by doing nothing energetically, Hoover could help his powerful industrial friends who could later help make him President.

None of this, or course, was planned just that way. It only looks so well organized from a distance. However, from this distance, certain discrepancies can be observed between Secretary Hoover's public statements about broadcasting and his actions. He claimed there was no advertising on the air and that no station was planning to do anything like sell time when he could not have been ignorant of AT&T's sponsored announcements and broadcasts over WEAF. Nor could he have been ignorant of the effects upon other stations when he moved WEAF to a clear channel, away from interference. While stating emphatically that the public air waves were not private property, Secretary Hoover nonetheless recognized the sale of broadcast licenses as private property. Although he claimed to admire

Herbert Hoover was Secretary of Commerce during all the pattern-setting days of broadcasting. This is a 1922 publicity photograph showing him listening through the earphones of one of the earliest radio receivers through which the human voice could be heard. (Wide World Photos)

the desire of the broadcast industry for regulation, somehow or other, at annual Radio Conferences, his resolutions went on record side-tracking any such regulation.

At a time when he could have strongly called the attention of Congress to broadcasting problems and either stimulated or helped sponsor legislation that would be fair, equitable, and protective of the interests of small, independent stations, particularly the nonprofit ones owned by churches, colleges, and universities, he either did nothing or actively helped industrial interests. Congressmen who presented radio bills were ignored, their bills pigeonholed, and they were pressured against making waves by those whose philosophy was industry-oriented.

As stated earlier, these moves were not blueprinted. They only look carefully planned from a distance. Since making money and exerting political influence took place on a day-to-day basis, politicians and industrialists had to do what they could to fit unexpected events into their over-all goals. Two such unexpected events were the start of World War I and the direction in which broadcasting developed after World War I.

The Navy took official control of all wireless facilities in 1914, and radio emerged from World War I in better technological shape than it had been in when the war started. Inventors such as Marconi, de Forest, Fessenden, Alexanderson, and others, combined with General Electric, Westinghouse, and other companies, temporarily shelved their industrial battles and, with the Navy's blessing and help, continued experiments to achieve clear transmission over long distances for wartime uses. At the conclusion of the war, when the political and industrial battles started again, we have seen how patent infringement suits hampered the manufacture of radios, how AT&T–GE–Westinghouse created RCA to hold patents for them and to sell receivers while AT&T sold transmitters.

One of the several ideas behind the 1919 agreements between Westinghouse, GE, and AT&T (described earlier in this chapter) was that a few transmitters strategically located and connected would serve the needs of the country. The companies, of course, would own the stations. To fulfill this part of the plan, each of the three companies was building its network, or "chain" of stations, as they were then called, as fast as it could while AT&T refused to sell transmitters. We have seen how this refusal inhibited no one.

While the general public listened breathlessly to the miracle of voices out of the air, to music, to political speeches, to advertising messages, to news reports, the hundreds of radio stations haphazardly grew into a large new industry. As far as the three companies were concerned, particularly AT&T, these independent broadcasters were infringing upon their "rights," and something had to be done. Although the situation looked different by 1924 from that envisioned in 1919, the whole plan would not be lost if the group reassessed broadcasting and what could be done with it.

While these thoughts percolated through executive offices, RCA officials learned that AT&T's subsidiary, Western Electric, was not only making home radio receivers, but was also undermining RCA's public relations efforts in Washington. According to the original agreements, RCA "owned" the market for radio receivers made of GE and Westinghouse parts. This was a double-cross by their own partner.

All these circumstances called for reorganization. The following elements represented the national situation when representatives of all the companies involved in the agreements started secret meetings in New York:

1. GE, Westinghouse, AT&T, and RCA each owned a chain of broadcast stations, with AT&T's 26-station network spanning the country.

2. AT&T's network was making money successfully with "toll," that is, sponsored, broadcasting. Such program sponsorship was much as we know it today.

3. Hundreds of individual stations were operating throughout the country, owned by such diverse elements as established churches and Aimee Semple McPherson's evangelical Temple in Los Angeles; by millionaire hobbyists like Col. Edward H. R. Green, whose station, WMAF, broadcast from South Dartmouth, Mass.; by over two hundred educational institutions that offered general information and some credit courses over the air on a nonprofit basis; by resort hotels, manufacturers, department stores, newspapers, laundries, and other legitimate businesses, as well as by that old carnival fraud, the medicine man, who promoted mail-order "Elixirs of Life" and other phony miracle drugs over the air.

By 1924, then, no area of life was untouched by radio when the reorganization meetings started in deepest secrecy in New York.

During that same year, the Federal Trade Commission started an investigation of AT&T and its partners on charges of creating a monopoly and restraining competition by refusing to sell transmitters. At the same time AT&T brought a suit against station WHN, New York, on the old ploy of patent infringement. The charge was that WHN infringed upon AT&T's patents because WHN had not bought a license from AT&T in order to use transmitters for broadcasting.

Another lawsuit, instituted by the Department of Commerce that fateful year, brought to a boil licensing conflicts that had been simmering for several years.

In Washington, the Department of Commerce had been having a terrible time since the end of World War 1, trying to stretch the outmoded Radio Act of 1912 to cover a totally different kind of broadcasting from that for which it had been created.

First, the Department had to handle licensing. Beginning in 1916, hundreds of requests for licenses poured in. The Radio Act provided no means of screening applications, no way to ask the purpose of the station, nor any provisions for a refusal. As a result, everyone got a license, as we have seen. By 1924, metropolitan areas in particular became crowded. Thirty-eight stations operated in the New York area, for example, and 40 in the Chicago area.

Second, the Department had the problem of station power to decide about, even though there was no guidance in the Act. In the early 1920s, station power ranged from 1,500 watts at WGY, the General Electric home station at their Schenectady, New York, plant, the strongest at the time, to the hundreds of 5- to 500-watt stations scattered across the country. On its own, the Department decided that once a station was licensed at a certain power, that station could not increase its power without permission. As the numbers of stations increased, they interfered with each other, and many requested increased power to overcome the interference. However, this problem proved subordinate to the next.

Third, the Department wrestled with the problem of which channel during what hours each station of the hundreds could use, because the Act had allocated only one broadcast band to all licenses. This band, 360 meters or 833.3 kilocycles, was so overcrowded that stations wandered into other bands, broadcasting almost anywhere from 200 to 500 meters seeking clear air. In 1922, Secretary of Commerce Hoover gave permission to a few "powerful, well managed stations" to use the 400-meter channel (750 kc.) and to the weaker ones, permission to spread out a little in the 200-meter channel—which they all had been doing already.

By 1924, several national Radio Conferences had been held, in Washington or New York, convened by Secretary Hoover. Although the members of the broadcast industry announced plans for much that was of value to broadcasting and repeatedly asked for more realistic government regulation than the 1912 Act provided, these Conferences seem to have served the same function that the Department of Commerce's permission about broadcasting channels served—to give official sanction to what was already being done—although the Conferences had no legal powers. A major example concerns advertising on the air. Each time a Radio Conference was held, the industry representatives voted resolutions to approve the amount of advertising already on the air.

The Conferences were also occasions for government officials and industry executives to make portentous, sanctimonious, against-sin, in-favor-of-apple-pie-and-mother public relations statements about the purposes of broadcasting. Every possible ideal was pulled into the service of broadcasting—moral, cultural, familial, patriotic, and educational—but nothing was ever said about the purpose of broadcasting to make money and exert political influence, although that, in fact, was its major thrust.

One of the items of supposed self-regulation that was yearly put into resolutions at the National Radio Conferences in the early 1920s was a series of "gentlemen's agreements" about getting on and off the air in the stations' one channel. Each station in a given area agreed to broadcast during a certain time span, then sign off so that another station could take its place. However, if Station X was broadcasting a political speech that Station Y objected to, it was possible to interfere with the broadcast. Or if Station Z had a profitable broadcast going, extending into some other station's time, Station Z just didn't get off the air. Or if an independent station was allocated a few hours a week broadcast time while a station in one of the "chains" got the rest of the week's time, the independent requested more time or increased power or another channel—all of which were either refused or led to long, drawn-out, expensive hearings in the Department of Commerce offices in Washington. A Department denial of a request for a different channel by Chicago station WJAZ, owned by Zenith, which had objected to only two-hours-a-week broadcast time while KOA,

Denver, the GE station, had the rest of the week, led to total confusion on the air.

When WJAZ moved to another channel and increased its broadcast time despite the ruling, the Department of Commerce started legal proceedings, and the Attorney General ruled that the Secretary of Commerce was exceeding his powers according to the Radio Act of 1912 by allocating channels, broadcast time, and electrical power, and by denying requests for licenses—in fact, everything the Department had been doing for five years. This ruling started a two-year period of wholesale channel jumping and "air wave piracy," during which two hundred new stations were started. Stations shifted all over the dial, with the best financed ones increasing their power in 1,000-watt leaps. All changed broadcast hours at will. The small stations either closed down or sold their licenses to larger ones. During these two years, noncommercial stations practically disappeared. Some church stations traded licenses for free time on Sunday mornings. College and university-owned stations either sold their licenses to private companies or stopped broadcasting.

Also during these two years—1924–1926—the corporation meetings in New York moved from climax to climax, charge to countercharge, maneuver to maneuver, until agreements were reached in June, 1926. During the same time, the AT&T vs. WHN case was settled out of court, and the Federal Trade Commission's restraint of trade hearings lumbered on to no conclusion.

For the general public, during these two years, despite channel jumping and other confusions on the air, a new entity, "the radio star," emerged. Thousands of people heard broadcasts of events from the floors of both political parties' national conventions, even more heard a Presidential inauguration for the first time, and the broadcast of sporting events and entertainment began to settle into a routine.

After two and a half years of negotiations, the following were the major areas of agreement that AT&T, GE, Westinghouse, and RCA reached:

1. AT&T got control of network relays, both wire and wireless, for radio and television. (By 1926, television had been successfully tested in laboratory experiments and could be seen taking its place as part of broadcasting.)

2. RCA got all broadcasting rights. Although it bought WEAF and that station's idea of sponsored programs, it had to lease all its relay lines from AT&T. In fact, everybody had to, whether or not they were involved in these or any other agreements.

3. All the companies could manufacture and sell transmitters and sound motion picture equipment. Manufacture and sale of home radio receivers remained in the hands of GE, Westinghouse, and RCA.

Thus AT&T bowed out of active broadcasting, but left its two main ideas in RCA's hands for development—commercial sponsorship and strategically placed stations linked into national networks. AT&T continued to control the means of broadcasting—wire and wireless facilities.

Following acceptance of the final agreements, RCA, GE, and Westinghouse formed the National Broadcasting Company, with RCA, now an independent company, the majority stockholder. On November 15, 1926, a four-and-a-half-hour broadcast over a 25-station, coast-to-coast network, featuring music, humor, and eulogies, launched NBC and the network era in broadcasting—one that is in existence today.

With a "red" network radiating from the old AT&T station, WEAF, and a "blue," from its original station, WJZ, the Radio Corporation of America, David Sarnoff at its head, established the dominating pattern of American broadcasting. By the mid-1930s, local programs had almost completely disappeared from the air as station after station tied into a network, broadcast "national" programs, and sold local time.

What happened to the AT&T–WHN case and the Federal Trade Commission's restraint of trade charges? WHN knew it couldn't fight an organization like AT&T and settled out of court, agreeing to pay a license fee and monthly charges for the use of telephone relay lines. Two-hundred and fifty other radio stations did the same thing for years.

Nothing conclusive was ever done about the Federal Trade Commission's investigation, which was dropped in 1928. The realignment of corporate agreements was evidently considered sufficient dispersal of assets, and, after the Radio Act of 1927 went into effect, RCA used the old patent ploy on its competitors, Zenith, Atwater Kent, Philco, and the others, allowing them to buy licenses and pay RCA a percentage of their yearly income to compete.

In mid-1926, forces other than corporate were also on the move. The court decision about the Secretary of Commerce's lack of power under the Radio Act of 1912 was confirmed in July; channel jumping, increases in station power, changes in broadcast time, founding of new stations increased weekly, as did pleas, requests, demands for a radio law from the public, people within the industry, and the lawmakers themselves, including the President.

The Radio Act of 1927, which became law in February, was the final result of nine versions debated in Congress. With a few technical changes but no shift in philosophy, this law was incorporated into the Communications Act of 1934, when for primarily administrative reasons, all foreign and domestic communications were brought together under one agency. It is the latter law by which the Federal government "regulates" a broadcast industry whose pattern was firmly molded before the law existed.

The philosophy underlying the Communications Act includes the following features:

1. The air belongs to the people as a natural resource; therefore, it can be used, but not owned, by individuals for "public service."

2. "Service" must be equitably distributed—an idea that has been given widely divergent interpretations.

3. Requests for broadcast licenses must be properly screened. Congress did not think in 1927, as it did in 1912, that everybody who wanted one was entitled to a broadcast license.

4. Although the government's power is not absolute, it can "regulate" broadcasting, depending as guidelines on the "public's interest, convenience, and necessity." That last is the best known phrase of the whole Act. It has been waved over as many different situations as the flag itself. The number of things that the public never imagined to have been declared vital to its "interest, convenience, and necessity" are matched only by those the public never knows about that are, indeed, in its "interest, convenience, and necessity." What the public receives in its "interest, convenience, and necessity" is always decided by the basic combination of money and political influence.

The following are among the 1927–1934 Acts' reassurances to the public:

1. Broadcast licenses were to be granted for limited periods. The period today is three years, at the conclusion of which time each licensee must apply for renewal, giving the Federal Communications Commission opportunity to consider its broadcast record and a chance for public "challenges" to the renewal.

Until the upheaval in the militant 1960s, challenges to license renewals were almost unknown. Between 1934 and 1962, the FCC refused to renew only nine licenses. When challenges came, they proved strange and shocking to broadcast executives. Here, too, the desire for change had little to do with broadcasting, but a great deal to do with money and political influence. To date, the number of nonrenewals is under 20. The militancy of the 1960s stemmed from two sources: from minority groups such as Black, Chicano, and Women's Liberation groups, all protesting lack of professional opportunities; and from two successive Republican administrations, protesting media bias.

As we have seen in newspaper history, conflict between news gatherers and government officials is as old as mankind, but today, for the first time in mankind's history, the media as an entity, including conglomerates of both print and electronic, has grown to a gianthood large enough to fight toe to toe with the Federal government. Epic moments in the continuing battle include the 1969 attacks of Vice President Spiro Agnew on the news media and the 1972 White House revenge tactics on the Washington (D.C.) *Post*'s exposé of White House officials' involvement in the burglary of the Democratic Party's Presidential Campaign Headquarters in the Watergate office building, and the revelations it triggered. Challenging renewal of licenses to television stations owned by the Washington *Post* in Florida was one aspect of those tactics.

Most of the challenges in the 1960s made by representatives of minority groups were averted by station owners who agreed to hire a certain percentage of people from Black, Chicano, and other groups, as well as to run programs and news that included favorable representation of minority groups. Advertisers quickly adopted a policy of including Black families in their detergent, patent medicine, beverage, and food commercials in both print and electronic media.

2. The Act reinforced the right of free speech against censorship, except for "obscene, indecent, or profane language." Enforcement, of course, always depends on what language use is currently acceptable.

3. Action against monopolies was built into the Radio Act by forbidding licenses to any person, corporation, or subsidiary that had been found guilty of monopolistic practices and to circumvent telephone company control. Special regulations were supposed to be made to cover network operation. Unfortunately, none of this has ever been applied practically. AT&T was in control of the means of broadcasting before the 1927 Act was created, the network era had already started, and no licenses have been withheld or revoked because of monopoly. Monopoly has become "the American way of life."

Neither the Radio Act of 1927 nor the Communications Act of 1934 mentions advertising; therefore, no regulation exists of types of commercials, level of sound, or number per hour broadcast. "Over-commercialization of the air waves" has been an issue debated and discussed, protested and defended, clucked over, deplored, or wept about by all concerned since the beginning of radio. The rhetoric on both sides has been magnificent, flags and ideals have been waved vigorously, but the only change ever made has been to increase the amount and the impact of advertising on the air. Any type of legal regulation has been so skillfully blocked that, to the citizens most concerned, the subject might just as well have never been raised.

In both 1927 and 1934, efforts were made to give educational stations the protection of law, but they failed. The one in 1927 was so feeble that it is hardly worth mentioning, but the group behind the 1934 movement was stronger and better organized. They asked that 25 percent of the available broadcast channels be reserved for nonprofit making stations. The Congressmen involved gave the amendment the old college try, but the result was the same as in 1927. Nothing doing. It wasn't until almost 30 years later that the political climate permitted passage of laws supporting educational radio and television stations on FM and UHF bands.

The administration of the Communication Act of 1934 was placed in the hands of a seven-man Federal Communications Commission. These were and still are political patronage appointees, as they were under the original Radio Act of 1927. In 1927, the group had only five members and was called the Federal Radio Commission. The first five were chosen by Secretary of Commerce Herbert Hoover, which should indicate their connections, loyalties, and philosophy. The order they brought out of the chaos was industry oriented.

The Commission was originally supposed to exist for a year to straighten out the mess broadcasting was in and to reduce the number of stations on the air. However, the ramifications of their job seemed to increase year by year, and year by year, the Commission's life was extended until it was made a permanent fixture of government.

The length of time in office varies for each FCC member so that everyone won't be replaced the same year. However, the length of time the Commission Chairman stays in office seems to depend upon the vigor with which he exerts effort for those people both politicians and industry executives are always talking about—the public that is supposed to own the air waves as a natural resource. The more vigor he exerts, the shorter his tenure.

In the pattern-setting days of the electronic media, the position of the Federal Radio Commission appeared to be that of an undernourished stepchild in an affluent family, a Cinderella whose Prince Charming never appeared. The financially restricted Commission was supposed to wield extraordinary powers of regulation over a very rich and powerful group with many ways of its own to exert political pressure. The Commission had only one means of enforcing regulations—refusal to renew license. The record of the number of nonrenewals indicates clearly how active the Commission has been in this area.

The area in which the Commission was, and still is, most active is in establishing technical and engineering standards. Concomitant with their efforts to reduce the number of stations stumbling over each other on the air, the Commission sought to update and supervise use of equipment. Their record in this area has been outstanding. There are, however, interesting questions to ask about what happened to FM radio broadcasting and UHF television broadcasting. Use of both these bands, as equipment was developed to make them available, could have substantially increased the number of stations on the air and extended the electronic media into neglected areas, but they have not been so used.

The pattern-setting days for all practical purposes, therefore, ended in 1927 when the resources of private, exclusive, corporate agreements created a combination of networks and advertising that took control of the country's broadcasting outlets. The appearance of Columbia Broadcasting System in 1927 to compete with RCA's two NBC networks seemed sufficient "free enterprise" for years, until the government finally required NBC's Red and Blue networks to divide into NBC and ABC.

Three national networks, then—each operating both radio and television, with policies, programs, personalities, and advertising practically interchangeable, so alike are they—apparently satisfy all requirements of competition in a free society and all the ideals of democracy because that's the way it is today. The advent of FM, UHF, and government-supported educational broadcasting created a few poor relations to the three networks, but they, too, adopted the basic pattern of broadcasting that was set in 1927 and is on the air today. The few additional regulatory powers given the FCC recently and the few antitrust cases brought against the media generally since 1930 have had practically no visible effect. You see and hear the same pattern of broadcasting as did your grandparents. The only changes in content have been those of language and attitude that changed first in the general culture of the country.

Activities

1   Report Topics
Either by voluntary choice or assignment, individually or in groups of two or three, investigate the following subjects. Report your findings in appropriate combinations of narration, tapes, recordings, still photographs, and sound film.

A.   Current controversies—Who is the broadcasting industry fighting with and what about? What are the latest FCC investigations, proposals, rules and regulations? Are there any individuals in broadcasting in difficulty with any organization or any part of the government?

B.   Federal Communications Commission—Who is the current Chairman? What are his viewpoints about his job and the various aspects of broadcasting? Who else is currently on the Commission? Has a woman been appointed to the Commission? Are there any members from minority groups? What is the Commission currently doing?

C.   Legal powers of the Federal Communications Commission—Apart from license renewal, identify the legal powers of the FCC. What laws have been enacted recently pertaining to media ownership, political broadcasts, equal time for opposing politicians, and rights of broadcasters to editorialize? What is the legal strength of FCC Rules and Regulations?

D.   Challenges to license renewals—Have there been any recent challenges to a station's license renewal? On what grounds? Who brought the challenge? For what purposes? What major challenges took place in the last few years? What were the dispositions?

E.   Status of women in broadcasting—Who, what, and where are the women in broadcasting? Check local stations to discover what top management jobs are held by women.

F.   *Educational broadcasting*—What's happening on your local Public Broadcasting Service station? What is the current status of Federal funding for the Corporation for Public Broadcasting? Any conflicts in this area in Washington, New York, or other major centers? What is the contemporary political attitude locally and nationally toward educational broadcasting?

G.   *High points and low points in broadcasting*—Following are a few of the high and low moments in broadcasting. Choose items from each, or create your own lists, for an objective report on balance and ethics in broadcasting.

High Points	*Low Points*
Kefauver Crime Investigation Committee hearings broadcast, 1951.	Bribery of quiz program contestants such as those on "$64,000 Dollar Question."
CBS-TV "Playhouse 90" dramatic series in 1950s.	Payments (Payola) to disc jockeys to play certain records.
Edward R. Murrow and Fred W. Friendly's TV series, "See It Now."	Network censorship of program scripts such as those of the Smothers Brothers program.
Army-McCarthy hearings broadcast in the 1950s.	Neglect of vital public issues in favor of old situation comedy reruns.
First man on moon broadcast in the 1960s, as well as all other moon shots.	Television rules for broadcasting football, basketball, hockey, tennis, and other games.
Broadcasts of outstanding dramatic and musical performances.	Amount of violence on television.
Documentaries such as the "Jacques Cousteau" series of underwater investigations.	Low quality of children's programs.
Broadcast of series such as "Wild Kingdom" and "Survival."	Over-commercialization.
Broadcast of the Senate Committee's hearings on the Watergate break-in.	Poor quality of daytime television programs.

2   *Cultural Comparisons*
    Using the collected tapes and records of radio programs broadcast during radio's Golden Years and tapes made of contemporary programs of

the same kind, compare differences and similarities of life as presented on the electronic media. How do comedy programs such as Fibber McGee and Molly, Fred Allen, Jack Benny, and other situation comedies compare with those popular today? Is what was funny then the same as what is funny now? In what ways are "The Shadow" and "Mr. District Attorney" the same as, and in what ways different from, current law enforcement and detective series? Can you identify changes in attitudes and language between then and now? What conclusions can you reach about trends in programing on the basis of this data?

3   Discussion and Debate Ideas

The electronic media, particularly television, offer subjects for almost endless discussion and debate. The following ideas are suggested topics for informal class discussion or formal debates, or they may be used to stimulate ideas of your own:

A.   The material broadcast on radio and television is mainly entertainment, and entertainment does not exist to be analyzed.

B.   One of the early fears about programs originating mostly from big cities and talent centers such as New York and Hollywood was that regional music, dancing, and humor would be forgotten. This fear has come true. Even regional accents are disappearing because America has been homogenized by the electronic media.

C.   A broadcast station provides its community with a means of self-expression, giving its listeners a broadcast voice, as well as asking for the community's ear.

D.   Take a position on one of the following statements and provide documented support of it:

(1) Broadcasting is varied, educational, cultural, and magnanimous.

(2) Broadcasting is venal, boorish, tiresome, and corrupt.

*A friend of mine runs a clipping service whose staff looks
every day at every page of every daily newspaper
published in the United States. . . . [In] a paper of more
than fifty thousand circulation . . . he found that 82
percent of the paper's nonadvertising matter—local, wire
and syndicate—originated completely, or virtually
completely, with the news source itself.*

Ben H. Bagdikian
The Effete Conspiracy

*Thirty years ago we elected presidents with colorless
personalities and poor voices, but today the public places
high value on such assets as convincing speech and an
ability to project individuality.*

Hardie Albright
Acting: The Creative Process

Chapter 7
Publicity and Propaganda in the Media

Advance Preparation

1. Either by volunteer selection or assignment, call each newspaper, radio, and television news department in the area and ask that publicity releases and press handouts be saved for a week. Ask them to keep those not used as well as those used, if possible. Pick up the collection from each source at the end of the week.

2. Arrange for speakers from the Public Relations offices of large businesses, public service organizations such as Red Cross, and government offices. Follow them with editors and reporters from the news media.

3. Prepare questions for each speaker. Ask PR people how they inform or "educate" the public about their organizations. Ask media people how they use the material they receive.

The Reputation of Journalism

After the age of image-making and publicity reached full growth following World War II, the work of public relations directors, departments, and agencies; of publicity and lobbying organizations; and of other well-heeled pressure groups, including the media themselves, caused a great deal of respect for journalism to vanish. Respect has been replaced by suspicion and disbelief, and a general feeling that in spite of overwhelming amounts of detail, the public is not given "real" information. Many people think that, by flooding the media with reams of unimportant details and using incomplete, slanted, and misleading data to hide important negotiations, manipulations, and over-lapping connections between members of Congress and the military and industrial complexes, this coterie of Press Secretaries, Public Relations Directors, and hundreds of lesser PR people have destroyed the reputation that responsible journalists had worked several generations to achieve.

Another reason for thinking that the information given the public is inadequate has been the decrease of competing news outlets. Concentration of ownership of the local newspaper, radio, and television station in one corporation doesn't make for competitive reporting. At one time not all that long ago, major cities supported from three to nine competing newspapers. By twos and threes, they combined or went out of business. At its peak, radio newscasting featured thirty to fifty news broadcasters and commentators who gave a variety of viewpoints. Television newscasting, unfortunately, is even more limited than contemporary newspapers, with three networks supplying all the news, and all of it sounding as though written by the same person.

During the era in which the newspapers were establishing their respectability and before the age of the publicity handout, the image of the ideal reporter as a godlike figure began to take shape and become part of American folklore. He developed into a fast-moving, fast-thinking, fast-talking, rough, tough, but courageous person; idealistic, unselfish and tenacious for the public good; able to strip away all pretense, hypocrisy and sham to right a wrong for the "little guy." The embodiment of this folk hero is Superman, the suprahuman personality of Clark Kent. a newspaper reporter. Brenda Starr is his feminine counterpart.

This godlike image of the reporter is renewed on television every time a well-known commentator or "anchor man" on a major network's prime time newscast appears, larger than life, in full color in your living room, his resonant baritone enunciating clearly, exactly, and emphatically "interpretations" of the news that may or may not be accurate or objective. To nonanalytical and uninformed people, he *could* sound like a voice from heaven uttering unquestionable truths.

Contemporary General Reporting—Publicity and Propaganda

"Propaganda" is a word that triggers disapproval. It usually is applied to politics because it acquired a bad reputation keeping company with politicians. Today, however, we live in a world so dominated by manipulative devices that it is difficult, frequently, to tell genuine information and propaganda apart, or to distinguish between a true event and one engineered by public relations and publicity people. No professional or amateur organization that deals with the public thinks it can reach its goal or even survive without the help of propaganda in the guise of "public relations" and "publicity."

To avoid stirring up disapproval almost automatically, no commercial organization or public service, no political or social enterprise would think of using the word "propaganda" except to describe what their competitors or opponents are doing. "We good guys," each modestly implies, "just want to tell our story. The public will then know the TRUTH and decide on their own how wonderful we are." Whether we accept their stories as factual or misleading, as the whole truth, part truth, or no truth at all, seems increasingly to depend upon our allegiances. If we support the organization, the ideas or ideals it proclaims, and believe in the people behind them, we accept the information as factual. If we do not, we claim the information is "just publicity," meaning fairly harmless, or "propaganda," meaning harmful.

Whereas advertising aims to create in you the irresistible urge to open your wallet, take out money, and hand it over in return for a product or service, publicists aim to create beliefs. The people engaged in publicity and public relations activities want you to live according to the beliefs they espouse mostly for their own benefit and the benefit of their employers. They always claim these benefits will be yours, too, and because of this, you should emotionally and financially support them. Your benefits from such support, somehow or other, always seem more indirect and less tangible than theirs. When this curious situation is pointed out, PR people immediately assure you that you will benefit in the long run. Meanwhile, you receive psychological rewards such as a sense of participation in important events, satisfaction of being among those who control the destiny of civilization, a sense of belonging to the in-group, and the warmth of being admired by those in government, particularly if you or members of your family voted for them.

Users of organized publicity range from giant monopolies made up of intertwining, mutually helpful, mutually exclusive corporations to small social clubs. Publicity for the former means power and profit; for the latter, a bit of icing on the cake of daily life when a member's neighbors notice a published item or picture. Far from last or least is use of publicity by both governmental agencies and individuals. Consider the following article:

Gurney's Role Is Untold

By TOM RAUM
Associated Press Writer

Republican Sen. Ed Gurney's role in helping Florida recover from Hurricane Agnes remains largely untold—despite his repeated attempts to tell it.

Gurney aides kept his long distance lines to Florida buzzing throughout last week with a steady flow of Gurney statements to newsmen about his feelings on the storm.

Mostly victims of bad timing, few of them ever made it into print.

For instance, Gurney's announcement that he had sent telegrams to city and county officials in 17 counties expressing "concern for hard hit areas" was upstaged by a helicopter tour of damaged areas of the state by junior Sen. Lawton Chiles, a Democrat from Lakeland, and Gov. Reuben Askew.

"Well, Sen. Gurney's telegrams were sent long before Askew or Chiles decided to make the helicopter tour," testily protested Eleanor Jordan, a press aide to Gurney.

The following day Gurney's office announced that he would assist in obtaining federal disaster funds for Florida—about the same time Askew's office announced that the governor would formally apply for the funds himself on Friday.

And on Friday Gurney's office called to say that he would attempt to expedite Askew's request, but he got upstaged this time by President Nixon's declaration of five states—including Florida—as disaster areas.

Gurney's office followed this up with a news release claiming he had "been in touch with county and city officials of areas hardest hit by the hurricane and has offered his assistance in helping officials get aid for their areas."

The U.S. senator from Winter Park wasn't the only official to crank out press releases on the storm. Agency after agency cranked them out assessing the storm's effects on everything from banks to unemployed workers.

And Hurricane Agnes apparently churned up latent literary yearnings in the soul of an anonymous Department of Transportation news release writer.

"Hurricane Agnes dealt a financial blow to the Florida Department of Transportation Monday as she flounced her soggy skirts around the state," began one handout on storm damage.

Another referred to "damages wreaked by the now infamous Hurricane Agnes."

Although written in a tongue-in-cheek manner, this article is factually accurate about the way publicity originates. In addition to illustrating political acrobatics known as "jumping on the bandwagon" and the callous use of the philosophy that "it's an ill wind that doesn't blow somebody some good," this piece of mild satire illustrates both political and governmental uses of media publicity. Statements, verbal and written, "cranked out" by both the Senator and "agency after agency," as noted in the article, did not blow in only upon the Associated Press, but they hit every media desk, much like the hurricane itself, from Florida to Massachusetts.

Although the basic purpose of publicity is self-seeking, much of it stems from a desire to give recognition to worthwhile programs, people, and activities. The following articles all represent publicity at the other end of the spectrum from the Florida Senator's:

Gwinnett Police Teach Civics

By BILL MACNABB

Gwinnett County police have launched a campaign to inform residents about their work and the business of county government.

An old school bus sporting a new look is being used as a Mobile Information Center.

While the project is aimed at newcomers to the county, comments from longtime residents show that the brief orientation on county government is attracting both groups of people.

The bus is painted beige on top covering the side windows and brown on bottom, the same familiar colors of the police squad cars.

Inside, one finds paneled walls and a carpeted floor with cabinets and displays on either side.

Through donations from local businessmen, the police held the cost of refurbishment to $550, according to Officer R. J. McFarland, head of the project.

McFarland said that in five unannounced trips to shopping centers and one political rally ("during a big rain storm"), the information center has attracted 300 people.

"Our plans are to try to keep the bus in the shopping centers on Fridays and Saturdays," McFarland said. "The rest of the week we'll take it to subdivisions and other cities in the county."

The tour of the center begins at the rear of the bus. A tape recording explains each display as the visitor passes through.

The taped message says that the center will attempt to reach many of the estimated 1,200 persons who move into Gwinnett each month.

The displays identify the county officials and explain their responsibilities.

One police display, housed in a glass case, shows different types of illegal drugs, including samples of many.

Visitors receive numerous brochures on topics ranging from drug abuse prevention to bicycle safety.

There is also a handout offering a complete list of emergency telephone numbers and phone numbers of each office in county government, naming the department head.

When a visitor reaches the front of the bus, he sees a plaque bearing the names of six law enforcement officers who have died in the line of duty in Gwinnett.

Three Gwinnett police officers were murdered in 1964, two Buford officers died in an auto crash while chasing a suspect in 1968 and a Suwanee officer was shot by a robbery suspect in 1965.

Officer McFarland said he's hopeful school officials will let students take time to visit the information center during the school year. "I think it will be helpful for students to learn about county government, especially the ones in civic classes," he said.

McFarland said the mobile center would also be available for display at civic club meetings upon request.

Atlanta *Constitution*, Aug. 3, 1972

58 Denver-Area Girls, Boys
To Compete in Soap Box Derby

A $500 savings bond and an all-expense paid trip to Akron, Ohio, will be on the line Sunday when 58 Denver-area youths—including nine girls will compete in the annual Denver Metropolitan Soap Box Derby.

Finals of the big race will be at 3 p.m. at Colorado Blvd. and First Ave. Time trials will begin at 11 a.m. The event is free to the public.

In addition to the bond and trip to the national derby Aug. 26, the winner will receive a trophy.

Other trophies will go to second and third-place winners, to the owner of the best-constructed racer and to owners of racers with the best brakes and the best upholstering. There will be a special trophy for the best sportsman.

The event is sponsored by the Exchange Clubs of Denver and the Denver Police Department.

Girls entered include: Bernadette Hale, 1701 Pierce St., Arvada; Judy Beveridge, 13555 W. Colfax Ave., Golden; Elizabeth Carpenter, 411 Balsam St., and Kathy Lantzy, 1030 Vance St., Lakewood; Kim Howard, 7147 S. Spruce St., Englewood; Carol Reid, 1245 W. 97th Ave., Debbie Knippath, 850 S. Fillmore St., Anita Bailey, 2295 S. Linley Court, and Luann Sanford, 4980 W. Vassar Ave., all of Denver.

Boys entered include: Richard, Robert and Russell Hale, 1701 Pierce St., Arvada; John Beveridge, 13555 W. Colfax Ave., Bob McInroy, 17211 W. 16th Ave., and Scott Orr, 13190 W. 30th Place, Golden; Robert and Scott Carpenter, 411 Balsam St., Mike Lantzy, 1030 S. Vance St., and Bob Lazori, 784 S. Hoyt St., Lakewood. . . .

Denver Post, July 30, 1972

Mile High To Honor Pam, Mom

Mile High Kennel Club officials have declared Monday "Pam Greene Night" at the Adams City greyhound racing track in honor of the 18-year-old Denver girl's qualification for the Olympic Games in Munich.

Miss Greene will compete in the 200-meter dash in the Munich Games.

Al Ross, president of Mile High, said that Pam will be given a specially-designed good luck charm bracelet and a greeting bearing the best wishes and signatures of the track's employes.

Pam and her mother, Mrs. Bertha Greene, will be honored guests for the evening and the entire racing program will be dedicated to her success in Munich.

Denver Post, July 29, 1972

The following article was written in one of two ways. The reporter, alerted to Sherwin's presence in St. Louis by the local club's publicity chairman, either interviewed the visitor or rewrote the article from material provided him from the Sierra Club's national headquarters. It is a typical example of "believe in us, good guy" publicity. Directly, the more such "news" the Sierra Club gets into papers and on the air, the stronger the organization's stand can become. Indirectly, it's a bid to increase the membership. Whether anyone pays any attention to the article depends upon personal allegiances.

Sierra Club Must Seek Victories In Congress
By E. F. PORTER JR.
Of the Post-Dispatch Staff

Notwithstanding its spectacular record of courtroom successes in recent years, the Sierra Club must begin to shift its defense of the environment to other fronts, the president of the 140,000-member conservationist organization believes.

Raymond J. Sherwin of Vallejo, Calif., the organization's president, contends the day of the environmental lawsuit, in which environmentalists square off against industries or Government agencies, is drawing to a close. As a theater of operations, the courtroom is going to be replaced by the congressional committee room and the school classroom, he said.

Sherwin, a trial court judge, was in St. Louis briefly last week to visit the officers of the local Ozark Chapter (Missouri and Arkansas). Part of his visit was devoted to a tour of the region's ecological hot spots, the Earth City development on Missouri Bottoms in west St. Louis County, the site of the proposed L-15 levee in St. Charles County and the site of the proposed Meramec Park Dam. The Sierra Club opposes all three.

Litigation by the Sierra Club and other conservationist groups has made "an imposing episode in the historical development of the law," Sherwin said. "The next thing is a legislative and educational program that will sustain these programs."

Sierra Club litigation has, for example, blocked timber cutting on federal lands, a nuclear power plant on Chesapeake Bay and federal approval of a state air pollution control program which would allow degradation of air quality. The club has been an intervenor in dozens of other lawsuits.

Industry is beginning to fight back, Sherwin said. The McKeon Construction Co. of Sacramento, Calif., has filed a $48,000,000 damage action against a Sierra Club member who blocked a rezoning proposal the company favored. The timber industry has sued the club itself for successfully forcing the National Forest Service to withhold cutting permits.

"It shows the extent to which members of various industries will go to intimidate the Sierra Club," he said.

"Moreover," Sherwin continued. "The results of litigation are likely to be temporary. All the National Environmental Policy Act (which has been the basis for many successful environmental lawsuits) does is force the government to stop, temporarily, and look at the alternatives to a project such as a highway or a dam."

"We must use this time to persuade the people politically that the project should not be done at all."

New weapons in the club's propaganda arsenal include informational books on specific environmental problems, school course materials and radio and television documentaries, Sherwin said. The club is seeking ecologically untainted corporations, like Xerox, to sponsor the documentaries, he said. . . .

St. Louis Post-Dispatch, July 30, 1972

One of the major ways PR people try to influence editors and reporters is the "freebie," a gift. This gift can range from a free lunch—sometimes on a daily basis—to large sums of money or pieces of personal property as lavish as a cabin cruiser. Large organizations pay media people's expenses for trips to "conferences" all over the world—Florida and Mexico in the winter, European and U.S. mountain resorts in the summer, major cities with famous restaurants, symphonies, and theaters at any time of the year. Gifts, in addition to all expenses being paid, range from cartons of the product to such items as cameras, jewelry, household appliances, sporting goods, clothing, cars, household furnishings, or anything else one might desire. The payment for such treatment is to write favorably and frequently about the product or organization and to refuse to write criticism of any kind and/or actively suppress it.

In the following article, substitute the names of any major company or group of companies in the country, change the reporters from those of the *Hoot Owl* to those of any medium or group of media, and you have the typical PR routine.

<h3 align="center">Kid Journalists Are Confronting
Freebies, Surviving</h3>

By JIM SCHUTZE
Knight Newspapers Writer

DETROIT—The kid journalists of the Hoot Owl, "America's First Newspaper for Children," are coming face-to-face with the freebie . . . and surviving.

That's no small contest. The freebie is what turns good reporters into hacks. It's free lunch, free car, free trip, free hotel, you name it: freebies are big and little goodies sometimes doled out to reporters by smart public relations people in hopes of getting favorable publicity.

The Hoot Owl, originally a protest against adult journalism, is a gutsy all-kid newspaper, written "by the kids, for the kids, about the kids." It started out two years ago in Arlington, Tex., with a circulation of 10. The paper now claims a national circulation of 426,000.

The average age of Hoot Owl staffers is 10 (the Hoot Owl enforces a mandatory retirement age of 16). Three hundred boys and girls around the country work as unpaid editors, correspondents and general assignment reporters.

MANAGING EDITOR Joey Edwards, 8, Environmental Editor Joel Turner, 13, and Science Editor Dewey Warner, 13, all of Arlington, were in Detroit recently to find out what the automakers are doing to increase auto safety and to decrease auto pollution.

The young editors are touring the country courtesy of Pepsi-Cola, General Motors and the Marriott Corporation, to "seek America."

Freebie No. 1: a comfortable lunch at Ford's world Headquarters with Ford public relations people and safety and pollution experts.

And more: the young journalists arrived in a stationwagon provided by General Motors. The hotel tab is being picked up by the Marriott Corporation. They're carrying sound and movie equipment donated by the GAF Corporation.

Monday, the kids ate well—and fired off tough questions between bites.

"Have you experimented with methane fuel or with electric or turbine engines?" Dewey Warner asked. "Have you produced prototypes of these?"

Jack Ninomiya of the Ford auto emissions office explained that Ford had indeed produced such prototypes but had found they cost too much to operate.

When Ford engineers told the boys that many anti-pollution devices cut down on engine efficiency, Joel Turner provided a counter-example from his own experience: "We have a '68 Plymouth that is an ex-North Carolina sheriff's car with the emission package and a four-barrel carburetor, and it gets 12 miles to the gallon."

"WAIT UNTIL you get your '72," said Public Relations Director Robert Heefty. "You'll get more like nine miles to the gallon."

Grown-ups take criticism from the Hoot Owl very seriously, according to grown-up co-publisher Dane Edwards, 35.

"When the paper recommended abolition of the (U.S.) Bureau of Indian Affairs (Headline: 300 years of White Man's Lies Has All But Destroyed The Red Man), we got good response from most people, but we got horrible pressure from the government," Edwards said.

Tallahassee *Democrat*, July 26, 1972

The way to identify publicity and public relations-inspired articles and photographs is to find the organization name. It doesn't matter who speaks for the organization, who is in the photographs, or whose activities are written about, the organization's public relations and publicity people either prepared the material, including the photographs, or set up the interviews and pulled together the people and props for the photographs. Every newspaper and magazine reporter and editor can attest to the almost unbelievable amount of material that comes in weekly from PR departments. In addition, telephone calls precede and follow the mailings. PR people will gladly and frequently explain to you, and anybody else who will listen, how they "work with the media" and "serve the needs of the people." They may even tell you how they "handle a bad story," that is, criticism about their company, such as a legal action being filed against it, orders from the Federal Trade Commission for it to recall a product, or revelation of one of its executive's misdeeds involving, say, political bribery. However, they usually act as though bad stories did not exist. There certainly wouldn't be any if the PR people could prevent it.

Some PR material can contain useful and interesting information, particularly if it deals with local people and actual events. Most of it, though, is blatant propaganda, designed to create a "we're the good guy organization, the corporation that cares" image and to promote sales or contributions by keeping their name before the public, if only by publishing the company's bowling team scores.

This kind of propaganda-through-publicity is harmless enough in general. At its best, it provides local people with recognition, and competent newspeople in the media throw out the advertising slogans and pages of flowery self-eulogizing. In addition, it provides jobs for large numbers of people in innumerable PR departments. These people know, if they have any journalism background at all, just how much of their "puff" pieces is likely to be used. (Handouts, press releases, and announcements are called "puff" pieces because they are full of hot air.) At the other end, in the editorial offices of the media, reporters and editors can sit comfortably at their desks, secure in the knowledge that the mail will be delivered and the telephone will ring and that they will never have to stir out of their seats except for lunch. Those who find this too inactive a life either get jobs in public relations to arrange the news, set up the events, and conduct the European tours for reporters—even with the penalty of having to write "puff" pieces—or go into teaching, which has its own rewards.

Activities

1. Look back at the reprint of the "Kid Journalists—Freebie" article. Who notified the press? At what event or moment in the tour did the reporter meet the people involved and get the direct quotations? What is missing from the article?

2. What organization provided the information about Pam Greene? What did it expect to gain from the publicity? What is its connection with Miss Greene? What actual expenditure of money was involved in setting up this "event"? What will take place at the "event"?

3. Look at both the "Soap Box Derby" and the "Teach Civics" articles. What organizations provided the publicity? What is the value to each organization of this kind of publicity?

4. Check through both a daily and Sunday issue of your newspapers and estimate how many publicity releases or public relations-inspired articles and photographs were used. What proportion of the total contents of the paper do they constitute?

5. Using the handouts and releases that the local press saved for you, match them with the articles that appeared in the paper. Note what was changed and how. What are the differences between the publicity release and the published article?

6. Pretend first that you are a public relations person; invent an organization and an event, then write the publicity for it. Now pretend that you are a reporter and rewrite the piece for a newspaper. Each type of writing is governed by many of the same requirements, but each has its differences. To be able to write both will require control of the appropriate elements of each.

Discussion

(1) What are your reactions to the uses of publicity by the print media? By the electronic media, whose practices are identical?

(2) What is left out of the newspapers because of their dependence on publicity?

(3) What is left out of press releases by public relations departments?

(4) What conclusions can you reach about the value of these practices?

Hard-Core and Benign Propaganda

Both hard-core and benign propaganda make use of the same formula as advertising: a dramatic appeal to emotion disguised as an appeal to logic that points the way to action. The purpose of propaganda is to convince as much of the public as possible to act for the benefit of the people issuing the propaganda.

The best examples of propaganda are usually found in politics, especially during election campaigns, whether national or local. The campaign ad shown on the following page was used in a high school campaign for student body president. It illustrates the following classic propaganda devices:

1. *Depreciation of the intellectual in favor of the practical*—Plain, practical people like you and me are better than intellectuals. Intellectuals, who deal in ideas, have heads full of cotton, hay, and rags, never get anything done, and are snobs to boot.

The bad-guy candidate is pictured on a pedestal speaking about ideas, which implies that he considers himself intellectually above the heads of the average students, socially their superior, and beyond reproach ("on a pedestal") in the bargain. The good-guy candidate has his feet firmly on the ground and, as a substantial citizen and practical fellow, is work-oriented.

2. *Use of generalities*—The good-guy candidate uses general, not specific, words. The work he will do for the students is not specifically stated nor are his objections to the other candidate's ideas. No one knows what either of them hopes to do for the student body, should he be elected. For all a student in the school can tell from this piece of propaganda in poster form, both candidates' platform might be the same.

The names on the boxes near the good-guy candidate are as non-specific as "Promises, promises, promises." They are all standard, general, basket-type words that carry different meanings for different people. Basket-type words are deliberately used in propaganda for exactly this reason. They allow a candidate to become all things to all people, he hopes. The student who is really concerned about "student involvement," for example, might think this candidate means he will formulate a plan and exert real effort to increase participation in service clubs. Another might think the candidate is going to arrange rallies to get more people out to ball games. Still a third might think he is going to "involve" more students in the work of the student cabinet. The candidate might have all these ideas in the back of his mind, but actually what he wants in the way of involvement at the present moment is to have students vote for him. Beyond that, who knows?

3. *Subtle, derogatory associations*—The reason for showing the good-guy candidate using the word "promises" is its bad association. A standard cliché of politics is that campaign promises are never kept. Even though the reasons why this word puts them off might never surface in the minds of the students who see this poster, somehow they feel there is something slightly unacceptable about vague "promises, promises, promises."

Another subtle, derogatory association is made by the way each candidate is dressed. The bad-guy candidate on the pedestal has his shirt hanging out and his hair is not only a little long but messed up, while the good-guy candidate's shirt is carefully tucked in, and his hair is not only neatly combed, but short.

In addition, the bad-guy candidate, to reinforce the "intellectual snob" image, is shown as thin, short, and wispy, while the good-guy candidate is taller, has a larger chest and more manly build, and, with his hand on his hip, evokes images of dozens of coaches and football players who customarily stand with their hands just like that. How better could the good-guy candidate in this propaganda poster set up the idea that the election pits a clean-cut, 100-percent, All-American athlete against an effete, intellectual snob?

4. Pointing with horror at the opposition doing the same thing you are doing: The good-guy candidate is saying, in effect, "How horrible it is to make promises that mean nothing and that you can't keep," and all the while he is doing the same thing. In this poster he is promising to "work" for the students. Who knows what that means and whether or not he will do it?

The total impact of this particular piece of political propaganda is subtle and emotional while appearing to be an appeal to logic, a logic so irresistible that the students cannot help but vote for the good-guy pictured. The same technique is used in all propaganda, no matter what form it takes: pictures, printed words, oratory, debate, documentaries—all of them.

A type of benign propaganda in general use today is that which appeals strongly to your pity and compassion while frightening you half to death in the name of a cause. The environmentalists use the technique by showing you dead birds and fish on the banks of polluted streams, or citing chilling statistics about the effects of smog and other kinds of atmospheric pollution. Your heart is wrung by the fate of the innocent creatures, and the statistics frighten you out of a night's sleep. Generally this kind of propaganda concludes with a direct or indirect appeal for funds to support an organization. These organizations range from those that "fight" pollution or incurable diseases to those that just want to do their own thing, whatever that may be. Whether or not you believe this particular kind of propaganda depends on personal viewpoints and allegiances. Some of the organizations unquestionably perform for the community's benefit; some exist just to perpetuate themselves. You take your choice and make your contributions accordingly.

The following article about the electrician combines all aspects of both publicity and benign propaganda. It was written and the accompanying pictures supplied by the public relations department of the organization being promoted. Although it is factually accurate, it is written as dramatically and emotionally as possible, and it was provided for publication during February, the month the organization conducts its nationwide campaign for financial donations. The organization's full name is mentioned twice; the indirect appeal for funds is in the next to the last sentence. Scare tactics are used throughout the emotional presentation, with the theme, "This can happen to you. Better contribute," underlying the whole article, but note how it concludes on an upbeat of hope.

The Voiceless Speak
By PEARL ALDRICH

Recently Edmund J. Maxwell, 711 Germantown Pike, spoke to a combined meeting of the Women's Auxiliary and the Men's Association of St. Mark's Lutheran Church in Oaklyn, N.J.

What makes this noteworthy is that Maxwell has no vocal chords. They were removed in 1946 because he had cancer of the larynx. Yet this speaking engagement is only one in a heavy schedule during which he visits and talks to thousands of people a year.

Like many another cancer victim, Maxwell felt his death warrant was signed the day he learned he had the disease. Up to then, life had been good. He had a good job as electrician with the Reading Railroad. He owned his home in Germantown, had a wonderful wife and two fine daughters. And there was nothing he liked better than his weekends of deep sea fishing.

At 45, an active outdoor man from his farm boyhood through his tour of Navy duty to the last few years of construction work before joining the railroad, he'd never had a sick day in his life. There was nothing the matter with him now except this strange, persistent hoarseness that for months came and went but now seemed to be with him for good.

One day in June of '46, when Ed couldn't speak above a whisper, a neighbor told him she was worried and wanted to ask her nephew, a doctor, about his condition. Weeks later Mrs.

Catherine Graven, 219 E. Durham St., admitted she was too frightened to tell Maxwell what she'd just read in an American Cancer Society leaflet—that persistent hoarseness is one of cancer's danger signals.

The doctor who examined Ed sized up the man before him, then said, "Can you take it? I think you've got cancer . . . but we can get it cured."

Ed was skeptical. As he put it, "I saw myself dead, flat on my back in a coffin in three weeks."

A week later he was flat on his back but in a hospital bed trying to realize he was alive but that his larynx had been removed, that he would never speak again, and that he would spend the rest of his life breathing through an opening at the base of his throat.

Ed's worst time was just after he came home from the hospital. His family took in their stride the fact that he had cancer because what first sounded like a death sentence was reprieved so quickly. But with all the love and good intentions in the world, the mechanics of living go on the same way and lifetime habits are difficult to break.

"Ed, do you think we ought to get . . ." wife Agnes would start to ask but stop in confusion when she remembered.

The telephone would ring and Ed would automatically pick up the receiver, then just look at it helplessly.

Or the children needed a word from their father. Half out of his chair, his mouth open to form the words, Ed would sink back, feeling futile.

As Maxwell described it, he felt like a ghost. Sure, he was alive but not part of living. It was all going on around him but he didn't fit.

Finally he remembered something his doctor told him in the hospital just after the operation. At the time, he was too confused to more than half listen. But now he recalled the doctor saying there was a method by which laryngects could learn to talk again. He called it "Esophageal Speech" and said Ed could talk if he could belch or grunt, then move his tongue to form words.

Sitting on the front porch, holding a newspaper or magazine as camouflage, sometimes taking a swig of ginger ale to help create gas in his stomach, Ed practiced for hours at a time, trying to burp or create a belching sound.

One afternoon he did it and within the next hour formed a word. "And I've been talking ever since," he says.

Although Ed speaks clearly now, with little apparent effort, it wasn't that easy. There were innumerable hours of trying. There was a little success at first and lots of failure. There was self-consciousness to overcome and learning to accept others reactions to his new voice—which sounds as though he were talking from the bottom of a well. Also, there was learning the mechanics of handling large words and long sentences.

But it was a happy day for the Maxwell family when, two months after he came home from the hospital wondering if life would ever be normal again, Ed reported to the Reading shops for work, talking enough to be understood.

Since then, Ed Maxwell has helped hundreds of laryngects speak again by teaching and encouraging those taught to teach others.

In 1951, he founded the Philadelphia Laryngects Association under a grant from the American Cancer Society and established the third group in the country to make an organized effort to rehabilitate laryngects.

Membership has now reached 325, and classes, which quickly outgrew the Maxwell living room, are held twice weekly at St. John's Church Annex on 13th St.

Because of his outstanding contribution to the community, Edmund Maxwell received the 1954 Benjamin Rush Award—known as "Pennsylvania's Nobel Prize"—given by the Medical Society of the State of Pennsylvania.

In addition, Maxwell takes an active part in the annual Cancer Crusade where his fund raising efforts are highly successful.

To everyone, Maxwell is a talking illustration of hope.

Philadelphia *Inquirer* Sunday magazine, *Today*

Activities

1. Keeping the political propaganda poster we studied in mind, look for other examples in either a current election campaign or a recent one. Look in the back files of newspaper and news magazines for the latter. How many of the classic propaganda devices can you identify? What other techniques did you find?

2. Using your newspapers, locate other articles of propaganda similar to "The Voiceless Speak." What fear is being played upon? What organization wants a contribution? Is that organization able to do anything about preventing or curing the fear it was stimulating? What value is that organization to the community?

3. Now that you have studied the practices of both publicity and propaganda, what are your reactions to them? What are your conclusions about their value in general?

General Conclusion Discussion Questions

(1) While analyzing print and broadcast journalism, you have no doubt noticed the large amount of crime news reported. This kind of reporting has become traditional over the years; so traditional, in fact, that few reporters and editors question its validity. The police beat is an old and honorable assignment for a reporter. Examine this tradition, noting in particular the crime stories in your papers, and answer the following questions:

(a) What public purpose does newspaper reporting of small robberies and assaults serve?

(b) Does this kind of exposure help or hinder the police?

(c) Does extensive coverage of trials help or hinder court room procedure and, in the end, justice?

(d) Could any of the crime reporting be eliminated without damaging the usefulness of the media?

(2) Another unexamined tradition of journalism is that "real" or "hard" news is news of a disaster. How valuable is disaster reporting in general?

(3) Censorship is a fact of today's existence, whether it is called "selection of news," "managed news," "protecting the security of the country," or "interpreting the news." What are your reactions to and suggestions about this situation?

(4) If the media are flooded today with the outpourings by publicity and public relations departments of material that each organization thinks is not only "safe" but profitable to release, what kind of information is not getting into the media?

(5) Check back five or ten years, discover the major upheavals and controversies being reported at that time, then try to locate reports of the same situations a year or two years later. Have things become better? Has recovery from disaster been accomplished?

(6) As a result of this close study of contemporary reporting, what are your reactions to the conditions of journalism today? What could be changed? What should be kept?

(7) As a class project, write, edit, and publish either on ditto or mimeograph what you can agree upon as the "ideal" newspaper, or put together the "ideal" newscast, using tape recorders and photographs.

Concluding Comment

Usually an author's concluding advice in a media textbook written for the public schools of our democracy is to point out ways in which conscientious citizens can influence change in the media. These ways include writing letters to the editors of newspapers and magazines, to the executives of the networks and local stations, and to members of Congress. In addition,' you are urged to join citizen groups, have seminars and discussions, and let your voice be heard in community activities.

All of these activities are great fun. They keep you active and involved. You can meet people and become known in the community. You can get married and divorced this way, as well as promote your own career or the careers of your children as they grow older. Politicians on the move make great gains participating in these community organizations, but little is accomplished in the way of bringing about change in the media.

Realistically, there are two effective ways to bring about change in the media:

1. Learn to identify their methods of manipulation, the emotion-triggering devices aimed at the predetermined response, and ignore them. Don't respond. Keep your hand in your pocket. Don't buy. Don't listen. Don't watch the program. Satisfy yourself, not others. Make judgments on the basis of objective comparisons, not hopes and fears.

2. Cultivate, develop, and exert political pressure on every level of government. Use every manipulative device on government that the media themselves use and get laws passed requiring the media to change.

The media respond only to financial and legal pressure, and that's what this book has been all about. There seems to be little difference between control by government, as in many parts of the world, or control by industry, as in this country. It is still control, with manipulation of the public as its aim. The ideal to be reached is a balance between industry and government control that actually does require the communications industry to operate in the public interest.

PRODUCING A MULTIMEDIA REPORT

Sound motion picture films and recordings are probably the most familiar multimedia presentations in school classrooms. In addition, all students are familiar with the illustrated lecture in which the lecturer stands beside a screen and explains the contents, meanings, references, and if appropriate, the symbolism of still photographs projected upon the screen. These materials are usually used by teachers to extend and enrich their subject.

However, in the past several years, multimedia reports by students themselves have become an increasingly popular assignment in many subjects, giving the students an opportunity to increase the variety of their experiences by synthesizing material from different sources and expressing their own ideas. Because the growing interest in combining electronic and print media makes designing, producing, and presenting multimedia reports an expanding area in education today, such reports are suggested as assignments throughout this text.

A major problem in producing multimedia reports is the difficulty in finding instruction in the technology required to present the material of a subject. To ease that difficulty, a few sources in media technology are provided here. They cover the basic elements needed for getting and using the multimedia report suggestions in this text. Additional information is available in most libraries under the old heading of "audiovisual aids" and the new heading of "educational technology." Under the latter, you will find subdivisions of "software," meaning the materials to be presented, and "hardware," meaning the machinery employed, such as projectors.

Even the beginner will know something about cameras, tape recorders, film strips, overhead projectors, transparencies, and various display materials just by going to school in today's culture; therefore, the first step is to capitalize upon this knowledge. A book of step-by-step instructions, such as the latest edition of a manual like Jerrold E. Kemp's *Planning and Producing Audiovisual Materials* (Chandler Publishing Company, Scranton, Pa., 18515), will show you all the procedures from idea to presentation. It gives instruction in using sophisticated commercial equipment as well as such homely techniques as dry mounting photographs with an iron and using a music stand for display purposes. Although published for use in teacher education classes, just skip the inspiration-and-uplift, all the little quizzes, and use the excellent detailed instructions. The book provides extensive bibliographies, incorporating both commercial and educational technology. This book, or one of the many like it, is an invaluable addition to a classroom reference shelf.

Producing a Multimedia Presentation, by Kathleen Dobberstein and Kathleen Drzick, is an interesting pamphlet that details Kathleen Dobberstein's personal experiences in designing and producing a mixed media presentation for her poem, "1960's: Decade of Muffled Drums," a commentary on the assassinations of John and Robert Kennedy and Martin Luther King. The booklet is available for approximately one dollar through the Michigan Council of Teachers of English, 401 S. 4th Street, Ann Arbor, Mich., 48103, or National Council of Teachers of English, 1111 Kenyon Rd., Urbana, Ill., 61801, Stock #45249.

The following magazines can provide helpful information for media production:

Media and Methods Magazine, monthly September through May, North American Publishing Co., 134 N. 13th St., Philadelphia, Pa., 19107. Although heavily oriented to cinema study, it provides useful how-to-do-its, reports, and sources.

A-V Communication Review, quarterly published by the Association for Educational Communications and Technology, 1201 16th St., N.W., Washington. D.C. 20036; for use by educators.

AV Guide: The Learning Media Magazine, monthly produced by Educational Screen, Inc., 434 S. Wabash Ave., Chicago, Ill., 60605.

Visual Communications Instructor, monthly published by Syndicate Magazines, Inc., 25 W. 45th St., New York, N.Y.

Media Mix: Ideas and Resources on Media and Communication, monthly September through May, published by Claretian Publications, 221 West Madison St., Chicago, Ill., 60606.

TRADE MAGAZINES AND PROFESSIONAL JOURNALS

In addition to the millions of words reviewing, analyzing, condemning, and praising the mass media in general publications sold on news and magazine stands, there are a couple of dozen magazines and journals devoted to serving the insiders. These are usually published by professional and trade associations, with their subscriptions being part of the annual dues. A few, however, such as *Editor & Publisher* and *Advertising Age*, are commercial publications that, over the years, have built up tremendous strength and prestige. Insiders in advertising, marketing, broadcasting, journalism, and public relations, as well as school teachers and college professors who prepare students to enter these worlds, look to trade magazines and professional journals for reinforcement, status, security, and reassurance that, regardless of the "slings and arrows" from the outside world, their inner, real world is stable and rewarding. These publications, therefore, are back patters for industry members, carrying mostly news of the profession, personal and company publicity, promotional material, all topped by a frothy, soothing editorial.

The one responsibly critical publication in the lot is *Columbia Journalism Review*. This journal staunchly maintains the pre-World War II philosophy that both print and broadcast journalism are supposed to serve the public, that reporters are supposed to tell the objective truth about events, that publishers and all the journalists they employ are supposed to be honest, and that all journalists are supposed to know the self-serving aims behind offerings of public relations people. Like Accuracy in Media, Inc., the small lobbying organization in Washington, *CJR* is a feather attempting to balance the whole weight of commercial journalism. Both AIM and *CJR*, unfortunately, suffer because their commentary always comes after the fact. Once in a great while, *Advertising Age*, the voice of the advertising industry, will print a critical editorial, but the magazine is mainly supportive.

The value of these trade magazines and professional journals to your study of the impact of mass media is the way in which they reveal the framework of values and beliefs that each segment of this interlocking industry works by, how they reinforce each other, and the contrasts they make when compared to the critical studies. Most of the publications on the following pages are available in libraries; some, like *Editor & Publisher*, *Variety*, *Advertising Age*, and *Billboard*, are sold on newsstands in large cities.

153

Advertising Age, weekly, published by Crain Communications, Inc., 740 Rush St., Chicago 60611, for advertising people.

ASNE Bulletin, monthly, published by American Society of Newspaper Editors, 1350 Sullivan Tr., Easton, Pa. 18042, for newspaper editors and ambitious reporters.

Billboard, weekly, Billboard Publications, Inc., 1 Astor Plaza, 1515 Broadway, New York 10036, for popular music record industry.

Broadcasting, weekly, Broadcast Publications, Inc., 1735 DeSales St., N.W., Washington 20036, for broadcast industry generally.

Broadcasting Yearbook, annual, Broadcast Publications, Inc., 1735 DeSales St., N.W., Washington 20036, for broadcasters and advertising people.

CATV Magazine, Communications Publication Corporation, 1900 W. Yale, Englewood, Colo. 80110, for people interested in cable television.

Columbia Jounalism Review, bimonthly, Columbia University, Graduate School of Journalism, New York 10027, for people in print and electronic journalism industry.

Communication: Journalism Education Today, quarterly, Journalism Education Association of U.S., Inc., Box 884, Springfield, Mo. 68501, for high school teachers.

Editor & Publisher, weekly, 850 Third Ave., New York 10022, for newspaper reporters, editors, and publishers.

Educational Broadcasting Review, bimonthly, National Association of Educational Broadcasters, 1346 Connecticut Ave., N.W., Washington 20036, for people in educational broadcasting.

Federal Communications Commission Reports, weekly, U.S. Superintendent of Documents, Washington 20402, for people affected by and interested in actions, investigations, and statistical compilations of the FCC.

Infinity, monthly, Society of Photographers in Communications, 60 East 42nd St., New York 10017, for professional and student photo-journalists.

Journal of Advertising Research, bimonthly, Advertising Research Foundation, Inc., 3 East 54th St., New York, 10022, for research departments of advertising agencies, college professors and students of marketing and advertising.

Journal of Broadcasting, quarterly, Broadcast Education Association, Temple University, Philadelphia 19122, for college professors and students of broadcasting.

Journal of Marketing, quarterly, American Marketing Association, 222 S. Riverside Plaza, Chicago 60606, for research departments of advertising agencies, college professors and students of marketing and advertising.

Journalism Quarterly, quarterly, Association for Education in Journalism, College of Journalism, University of Minnesota, Minneapolis 55455, for professors and students of journalism.

The Listener, weekly, British Broadcasting Corporation, Broadcast House, London WIA, 1AA, for writers, producers, directors of entertainment programs.

Marketing Image, bimonthly, Bardo Publications, Inc., 19 W. 44th St., New York 10036, for marketing executives and sales managers.

Matrix, quarterly, Women in Communications, Inc. (Theta Sigma Phi, The woman's honorary society in journalism), 8305A Shoal Creek Blvd., Austin, Texas 78758, for women in journalism.

Nieman Reports, quarterly, Nieman Foundation, Harvard University, 48 Trowbridge Rd., Cambridge, Mass. 02138, for philosophers and policy makers in journalism.

PRQ, quarterly, PR Aids, Inc., 305 E. 45th St., New York 10017, for public relations personnel.

Public Relations Journal, monthly, Public Relations Society of America, 845 Third Ave., New York 10022, for public relations personnel.

The Quill, monthly, Sigma Delta Chi, the men's honorary society in journalism, 35 E. Wacker Dr., Chicago 60601, for men in journalism.

Quill & Scroll, Quill & Scroll Society, international honorary for high school journalists, School of Journalism, University of Iowa, Iowa City 52240, for high school students.

RTNDA Bulletin, Radio-Television News Directors Association, WKAR, Michigan State University, East Lansing, Mich. 48823, for broadcast journalists.

Television Age, biweekly, Television Editorial Corporation, 1270 Avenue of the Americas, New York 10020, for television network personnel.

TV Basics, annual, TV Bureau of Advertising, 1 Rockefeller Plaza, New York 10020, financial statements for advertisers and media sales personnel.

Variety, weekly, Variety, Inc., 154 W. 46th St., New York 10036, for all show biz people.

SELECTED BIBLIOGRAPHY

GENERAL

Agee, Warren K., ed. *Mass Media in a Free Society.* Manhattan: University Press of Kansas, 1969.
Casty, Alan, ed. *Mass Media and Mass Man.* New York: Holt, Rinehart and Winston, 1968.
Farrar, Ronald T., and Stevens, John D., eds. *Mass Media and the National Experience.* New York: Harper and Row, 1971.
Hood, Stuart C. *The Mass Media: Studies in Contemporary Europe.* London: Macmillan, 1972.
Larsen, Otto N., ed. *Violence and the Mass Media.* New York: Harper and Row, 1968.
Klapper, Joseph. *Effects of Mass Communication.* Glencoe, Ill.: Free Press, 1960.
Peterson, Theodore, Jenson, Jay, and Rivers, William. *The Mass Media and Modern Society.* New York: Holt, Rinehart and Winston, 1966.
Schramm, Wilbur L. *Mass Media and National Development: The Role of Information in the Developing Countries.* Stanford, Cal.: Stanford University Press, 1964.
Schramm, Wilbur L., and Rivers, William. *Responsibility in Mass Communication.* New York: Harper and Row. 1969.

ADVERTISING

Baker, Samm S. *The Permissible Lie: The Inside Truth About Advertising.* New York: World Publishing Co., 1968.
Borden, Neil H. *The Economic Effects of Advertising.* Chicago: R. D. Irwin, 1947.
Carson, Gerald. *Cornflake Crusade.* New York: Rinehart, 1957.
Della Femina, Jerry, and Sopkin, Charles, eds. *From Those Wonderful People Who Gave You Pearl Harbor.* New York: Simon and Schuster, 1970.
Diamant, Lincoln. *Television's Classic Commercials—The Golden Years: 1948–1958.* New York: Hastings House. 1971. (Contains complete scripts.)

Dirksen, Charles J., and Kroeger, Arthur. *Advertising Principles and Problems*. Homewood, Ill.: R.D. Irwin, 1973.

Gilbert, Eugene. *Advertising and Marketing to Young People*. Pleasantville, N.Y.: Printer's Ink Books, 1957.

Glatzer, Robert. *The New Advertising: The Great Campaigns from Avis to Volkswagen*. New York: Citadel Press, 1970.

Martineau, Pierre. *Motivation in Advertising*. New York: McGraw-Hill, 1957.

Packard, Vance. *The Hidden Persuaders*. New York: David McKay Co., 1957.

Ross, Wallace A. *Best TV Commercials of the Year*. New York: Hastings House, 1967.

Rowsome, Frank, Jr. *They Laughed When I Sat Down: An Informal History of Advertising*. New York: Crown Publishers, 1959.

Turner, Ernest S. *The Shocking History of Advertising*. New York: Dutton. 1953.

CONSUMERISM

Bauer, Raymond A., and Greyser, Steven A. *Advertising in America: The Consumer View*. Boston: Graduate School of Business Administration, Harvard University, 1968.

Bennett, Peter D., and Harold H. Kassarjian. *Consumer Education*. Englewood Cliffs, N.J.: Prentice-Hall, 1972.

Demby, Emanuel H. "Over-the-Counter Lifestyle." *Psychology Today*, April, 1972, pp. 75–78 and 110.

Engel, James F. *Consumer Behavior: Selected Readings from American Marketing Association Publications*. Homewood, Ill.: R. D. Irwin, 1968.

Garrett, Pauline, and Metzen, Edward J. *You Are A Consumer*. Boston: Ginn & Co., 1972.

Green, Mark J., ed. *The Monopoly Makers: Ralph Nader's Study Group Report on Regulation and Competition*. New York: Grossman, 1973.

Margolius, Sidney. *The Innocent Consumer vs. The Exploiters*. New York: Trident Press, 1967.

Nadel, Mark V. *The Politics of Consumer Protection*. Indianapolis: Bobbs-Merrill, 1971.

Nader, Ralph, and others. *Action for a Change: A Student's Manual for Public Interest Organization*. New York: Grossman, 1971.

———, ed. *The Consumer and Corporate Accountability*. New York: Harcourt Brace Jovanovich, 1973.

———. *Unsafe at Any Speed*. New York: Grossman, 1965.

———, and others. *What To Do With Your Bad Car*. New York: Grossman, 1971.

———. *Health Food: Facts and Fakes*. New York: Walker, 1973.

THE PRINT MEDIUM

Bagdikian, Ben H. *The Effete Conspiracy*. New York: Harper and Row, 1972.
———. *The Information Machines*. New York: Harper and Row, 1971.
Balk, Alfred, and Boylan, James, eds. *Our Troubled Press*. Boston: Little, Brown and Co., 1971.
Cirino, Robert. *Don't Blame the People: How the News Media Use Bias, Distortion and Censorship to Manipulate Public Opinion*. Los Angeles: Diversity Press, 1971.
Couperie, Pierre, and Horn, Maurice C. Trans. Eileen B. Hennessy. *A History of the Comic Strip*. New York: Crown Publishers, 1968.
Detweiler, F. G. *The Negro Press in the United States*. Chicago: University of Chicago Press, 1922.
Doig, Ivan and Carol. *News: A Consumer's Guide*. Englewood Cliffs, N.J.: Prentice-Hall, 1972.
Ford, James L. C. *Magazines for Millions*. Carbondale: Southern Illinois University Press, 1969.
Graham, Fred P. *Press Freedoms Under Pressure*. New York: The Twentieth Century Fund, 1972.
Gramling, Oliver. *AP: The Story of News*. New York: Farrar & Rinehart, 1940.
Grey, Elizabeth. *The Story of Journalism*. Boston: Houghton, Mifflin Co., 1969.
Gross, Gerald. *The Responsibility of the Press*. New York: Fleet Publishing Corp., 1966.
Karolevitz, Robert F. *Newspapering in the Old West*. Seattle, Wash.: Superior Publishing Co., 1965.
MacDougall, Curtis D. *Interpretive Reporting*. New York: Macmillan, 1957.
Morris, Joe Alexander. *UPI: Deadline Every Minute*. New York: Doubleday, 1957.
Mott, Frank Luther. *American Journalism*. New York: Macmillan, 1962.
———. *A History of American Magazines*. 5 vols. Cambridge: Harvard University Press, 1938–1957.
Peterson, Theodore. *Magazines in the 20th Century*. Urbana: University of Illinois Press, 1956.
Pollard, James E. *The Presidents and the Press*. Washington: Public Affairs Press, 1964.
Sim, John C. *The Grass Roots Press: America's Community Newspapers*. Ames: Iowa State University Press, 1969.
Stern, M. L. *Shaping the News: How the Media Function in Today's World*. New York: Pocket Books, Inc., 1974.
Talese, Gay. *The Kingdom and the Power*. New York: Bantam Books, 1970.

Wertham, Frederic. *Seduction of the Innocent.* New York: Rinehart and Winston, 1954. (This book led to the Comics Code and increased concern about violence in movies and TV.)

Wolseley, Roland E. *The Black Press.* Ames: Iowa State University Press. 1971.

THE ELECTRONIC MEDIUM

Barrett, Marvin, ed. *Survey of Broadcast Journalism 1970–1971: A State of Siege.* New York: Grosset & Dunlap, 1971.

Barnouw, Erik. *A Tower in Babel: A History of Broadcasting in the United States to 1933.* New York: Oxford University Press, 1966.

———. *The Golden Web: A History of Broadcasting in the United States 1933–1953.* New York: Oxford University Press, 1968.

———. *The Image Empire: A History of Broadcasting in the United States from 1953.* New York: Oxford University Press, 1970.

Bower, Robert T. *Television and the Public.* New York: Holt, Rinehart and Winston, 1973.

Briggs, A. *The Birth of Broadcasting: The History of Broadcasting in the United Kingdom.* London: Oxford University Press, 1961.

Brown, Les. *TV: The Business Behind the Box.* New York: Harcourt, Brace and Co., 1971.

Cantril, Hadley. *The Invasion from Mars: A Study in the Psychology of Panic Based on Orson Welles' War of the Worlds Broadcast.* (Complete script included.) Princeton: Princeton University Press, 1940.

Efron, Edith. *The News Twisters.* Los Angeles: Nash Publishing Co., 1971.

Emery, Walter B. *Broadcasting and Government: Responsibility and Regulation.* East Lansing: Michigan State University Press, 1961.

Epstein, Edward J. *News from Nowhere: The Selection of Reality in Television News Programs.* New York: Random House, 1973.

Friendly, Fred W. *Due to Circumstances Beyond Our Control.* New York: Random House, 1967.

Frost, S. E., Jr. *Education's Own Stations: The History of Broadcast Licenses Issued to Educational Institutions.* Chicago: University of Chicago Press, 1937.

Gordon, George N., and Falk, Irving A. *On the Spot Reporting: Radio Records History.* New York: Julian Messner, 1967.

Green, Maury. *Television News: Anatomy and Process.* Belmont, Cal.: Wadsworth, 1969.

Harmon, Jim. *The Great Radio Heroes.* Garden City, N.Y.: Doubleday, 1967.

Head. Sidney W. *Broadcasting in America: A Survey of Television and Radio.* Boston: Houghton, Mifflin, 1972.

Higby, Mary Jane. *Tune in Tomorrow: A Story of Soap Opera.* New York: Cowles, 1968.

Levin, Harvey J. *Broadcast Regulation and Joint Ownership of Media.* New York: New York University Press, 1960.

Schafer, Kermit. *Best of Bloopers: Radio and Television's Most Hilarious Boners.* New York: Avenel Books, 1973.

Schramm, Wilbur L. *Motion Pictures and Real-Life Violence: What the Research Says.* Stanford, Cal.: Institute for Communication Research, 1968.

———, and others. *Television in the Lives of Our Children.* Stanford, Cal.: Stanford University Press, 1961.

Skornia, Harry J. *Television and Society.* New York: McGraw-Hill, 1965.

———. *Television Broadcasting of News.* Palo Alto, Cal.: Pacific Books, 1968.

Small, William. *To Kill a Messenger: Television News and the Real World.* New York: Hastings House, 1970.

"The Story of Public Broadcasting: A Special Report." Reprinted from *Broadcasting Magazine,* 8 November 1971.

Wyckoff, Gene. *The Image Candidates.* New York: Macmillan, 1968.

PUBLICITY, PUBLIC RELATIONS, AND PROPAGANDA

Bernays, Edward. *Engineering of Public Consent.* Norman: University of Oklahoma Press, 1955.

Blumenthal, L. R. *The Practice of Public Relations.* New York: Macmillan, 1972.

Boorstin, Daniel J. *The Image: A Guide to Pseudo-Events in America.* New York: Harper, 1961.

Brown, James A. C. *Techniques of Persuasion: From Propaganda to Brainwashing.* Baltimore: Penguin Books, 1963.

Cutlip, Scott M., and Center, Allen H. *Effective Public Relations.* Englewood Cliffs, N.J.: Prentice-Hall, 1971.

Dichter, Ernest. *The Strategy of Desire.* Garden City, N.Y.: Doubleday, 1960.

McGinniss, Joe. *The Selling of the President 1968.* New York: Trident Press, 1969.

Markel, Lester. *What You Don't Know Can Hurt You: A Study of Public Opinion and Public Emotion.* Washington: Public Affairs Press, 1972.

Sorenson, Thomas C. *The Word War: The Story of American Propaganda.* New York: Harper and Row, 1968.

Stahl, LeRoy. *The Art of Publicity.* Minneapolis: T. S. Denison, 1962.

TEACHING RESOURCES

The following sources of teaching materials and information somehow resist any other category.

Sources of Prepared Educational Media

JEA Media Guide. Prepared by the National Curriculum Commission of the Journalism Education Association, it contains listings and sources of films about all phases of mass media. The first compilation was published in 1966, with supplements following at irregular intervals.

Rufsvold, Marget I., and Carolyn Guss. *Guides to Newer Educational Media*. Published by the American Library Association, this contains listings of catalogs of media on all subjects. The ALA publishes a steady stream of such helpful material.

Association for Recorded Sound Collections, Oakland University, Rochester, Michigan 48063.

Dime Novel Club, 1525 W. 12th Street, Brooklyn, New York 11204, for collections of Horatio Alger books and similar publications.

Film Library Information Council, 17 West 60th Street, New York 10023.

Newsweek Magazine Education Division, 444 Madison Avenue, New York 10022, and the local Bell Telephone office will provide materials on aspects of mass communications. These would also be useful in the propaganda section for analysis.

Tapes for Teaching, National Repository, University of Colorado, Boulder 80302.

Philosophy

Boutwell, William D., ed. *Using Mass Media in the Schools*. New York: Appleton-Century-Crofts, 1962. Also available through NCTE, Stock #46104.

Browne, Ray B., and Ambrosetti, Ronald J., eds. *Popular Culture and Curricula*. Bowling Green, Ohio: Bowling Green University Popular Press, 1972.

Donnelson, Kenneth, ed. *Media and the Teaching of English*. Reprint of *Arizona English Journal* by NCTE, 1970, Stock #45150.

Sources of Recordings of Radio and Television Programs

The January, 1974, issue of *Popular Culture Airwaves Bulletin*, a publication of the *Popular Culture Association* (Bowling Green State University, Bowling Green, Ohio 43403), contains a comprehensive list of archives and tape sale sources for radio and television. These include educational institutions, libraries, associations, and private collectors in every section of the country. Following are a few of the largest institutional collections, plus a few sources for old radio programs:

ABC Media Concepts, 1330 Avenue of the Americas, New York 10019, or 1001 N. Poinsetta Place, Hollywood, California 90046. (ABC network documentaries. Sales and rentals.)

The Best of Radio, Box 1692 B, F.D.R. Sta., New York 10022.

The Great Radio Shows, Inc., Box 254, Woodinville, Washington 98072. (Dramatic and comic radio tapes.)

The Grady School of Journalism, University of Georgia, Athens, Georgia 30601. (All the programs since 1940 submitted in competition for the George Foster Peabody Awards.)

Recorded Sound Section, Library of Congress, Washington, D.C. 20540. (Old radio broadcasts in collection.)

Mass Communications History Center, State Historical Society of Wisconsin, 816 State Street, Madison 53706.

Memphis State Radio Archive, Department of Speech and Drama, Memphis State University, Tennessee.

Northwestern University Radio Archive Project, Department of Speech, Northwestern University, Evanston, Illinois 60201. (20,000 items including some NBC material.)

Radio Reruns, Box 724 SR, Redmond, Washington 98052.

Radio Yesteryear, Box H, Croton-on-Hudson, New York 10520.

Radio Vault, Box 9032, Wyoming, Michigan 49509.

Remember Radio, Inc., Box 2513, Norman, Oklahoma 73069.

Library of Recorded Sound, Stanford University, Palo Alto, California.

Superscope Library of the Spoken Word, 455 Fox Street, San Fernando, California 91340.

Vanderbilt Television News Archive, Joint University Libraries, Nashville, Tennessee 37203. (Videotape collection of evening newscasts of the three networks since 1968. Monthly *Television News Index and Abstracts* published since 1972.)

APPENDIX

The following article, by Representative F. Edward Hébert of Louisiana, is reprinted in its entirety from the Congressional Record *for Wednesday, February 16, 1972.*

Mr. Speaker, it has been nearly a year since the nostrils of America's television audience were choked with the stench of the irresponsible, politically curious presentation disguised by the title, "The Selling of the Pentagon."

The odor has never faded as is witnessed by the most recent analysis published by Accuracy in Media, an independent organization which will not let the truth die.

And after 1 year of squeamish, pusillanimous explanations by the Columbia Broadcasting System, the truth continues to emerge. The following speaks for itself:

[From AIM Bulletin, Feb. 1, 1972]

CBS Replies to Critics' Questions About "The Selling of the Pentagon"

February 23 will mark the anniversary of the first showing of the CBS controversial documentary, "The Selling of the Pentagon." Claude Witze of the *Air Force Magazine*, Congressman F. Edward Hébert, Chairman of the House Armed Services Committee, and Accuracy in Media were among the severest critics of this program. On March 20, 1971, AIM sent a 7-page letter to Richard S. Salant, President of CBS News, asking for his comment on many inaccuracies or questionable points in the documentary. In our letter to Mr. Salant, we said that we agreed with a statement made by Roger Mudd in the broadcast, which said: "Nothing is more essential to a democracy than the free flow of information. Misinformation, distortion, propaganda all interrupt that flow." AIM said that "The Selling of the Pentagon" contained a great deal of misinformation and distortion. We wanted CBS to clear up the disputed points as quickly as possible.

CBS PROMISES COMPREHESIVE REPLY

On March 29, 1971, Mr. Salant replied to AIM saying that he had decided to wait for the myriad of complaints and charges to accumulate and then prepare a comprehensive analysis. He said: "When this analysis is completed and at such time as we determine its release is appropriate, I will include you on our distribution list."

Many months passed and no reply to the questions was forthcoming. AIM raised this with CBS from time to time. We urged our supporters to write to CBS to prod them into releasing the promised analysis. Finally, in December 1971, CBS informed us that we could find the long-awaited analysis in the Congressional Record for December 15 and December 17, beginning on pages E 13493 and E 13697. There was no press release, no announcement that CBS had met its critics head-on and had shown them to be wrong. No copy of the reply was sent to the principal critics. We all had to look it up in the Congressional Record, where it had been inserted by Congressman Ogden Reid, who said he obtained it from the president of the Radio-Television News Directors Association. The press has completely overlooked this latest word in the great controversy over the CBS documentary. It appeared that that was precisely what CBS wanted. The less publicity the better.

CBS ADMITS A FEW ERRORS

CBS does not claim to be infallible, but AIM's experience is that it will rarely admit an error. Mr. Salant appeared on TV on the night of March 23, 1971. to reply to the critics of "The Selling of the Pentagon." He said: "We are proud of 'The Selling of the Pentagon' and CBS News stands behind it." He said they could refute every charge of the critics who had appeared on the air—Cong. Hébert, Secretary Laird and Vice President Agnew. Nine months later, in the statement quietly slipped into the Congressional Record CBS admitted that not all of the criticisms could be refuted. For CBS that was quite an admission. That was why they sought no publicity for their statement, we believe.

CBS now actually concedes that five points of criticism were to some extent justified. It admits that the editing of one of the answers Assistant Secretary of Defense Henkin gave to a CBS question might not have conveyed accurately what Mr. Henkin actually said. CBS also admits that it was wrong in saying of defoliated areas that "nothing will grow there any more." It agrees that it should have mentioned that one of the Pentagon films it criticized was actually produced by CBS. CBS also concedes that it greatly exaggerated the number of offices in the Pentagon, and allows that it should not have used language that implied that it had to track down the Industrial War College team that was putting on a National Security Seminar in Peoria, Illinois.

In addition to these admissions of error, CBS makes *de facto* admissions of error in two other cases. In the broadcast. CBS had said that a still unpublished report of the prestigious 20th Century Fund had estimated real total spending by the Defense Department on public affairs at $190 million, compared with the budget figure of $30 million. CBS now concedes that the report of the 20th Century Fund had been published at the time the broadcast was made and that it contained no such figure. CBS tries to wriggle out of this embarrassing situation by showing that such a figure was used in some of the research done for the study. However, it was also clear that the figure was not used in the published study precisely because it could not be verified and the 20th Century Fund quite properly would not accept it as valid. CBS was therefore both wrong and unethical in foisting off such a figure on its unsuspecting audience and using the prestige of the 20th Century Fund to authenticate it.

The second *de facto* admission of error relates to the CBS charge that Pentagon expenditures on public affairs in 1971 were ten times the 1959 level. CBS now admits that the 1959 figure for public affairs expenditures was not comparable to the 1971 figure because different definitions for "public affairs expenditures" were used in these two years.

ARE THE ADMITTED ERRORS SERIOUS?

Yes. Three of them are quite serious. The improper editing of the Henkin interview, which CBS now concedes, was one of the objects of the heaviest attacks of the critics of the documentary. For example, Martin Mayer in the December 1971 issue of *Harpers* magazine said this about the editing of the Henkin interview: "This episode shows at least subconscious malice, a desire by the producers of the program that the man in charge of the Pentagon selling apparatus look bad on the home screen." Reed J. Irvine, writing in the August 10, 1971 issue of *National Review*, said that in editing the Henkin interview, CBS did more than make Mr. Henkin look bad. He stated in his reply to one of CBS's questions his justification for spending public money to inform the public of the reasons why we need national defense. Since CBS was clearly out to prove that such expenditures were wasteful, the mangling of the Henkin interview was necessary to make sure the viewers were not provided with any effective counter-arguments to the point CBS wanted to make.

CBS, of course, does not go very far in admitting that it might have done better by Mr. Henkin. Discussing the transposition of answers that Mr. Henkin gave to incorporate them as parts of answers of different questions, CBS says: "Upon review, one might judge that a fuller answer could have been broadcast by including, in the composite answer, the second sentence of the 'original' answer . . ." CBS concedes that editing involves subjective judgments and that others may disagree with the judgments of CBS. It insists, however, that in editing the Henkin interview its intent was to condense and clarify, not to deceive. The admission that it might have done better by Mr. Henkin is limited and grudging, but it is a step forward from the previous insistence by CBS President Frank Stanton that the editing was completely fair.

The two errors cited above relating to the amount of money the Department of Defense spends on public affairs are serious because in the documentary CBS placed a great deal of emphasis on the amount of money being spent on these activities. It used the false $190 million figure in comparison with the combined news budgets of the three commercial television networks, showing a graph on the TV screen that told the viewer that the Department of Defense spent more to tell its story to the people than all three networks spent to bring them the news. The exaggeration of the size of the Pentagon expenditures at the beginning of the program helped establish the important nature of the subject of the documentary.

The other three admitted errors are significant in that they cast light on the bias and carelessness of CBS. The bias is clearly shown in the incorrect description of the results of defoliation in Vietnam. The truth could easily have been ascertained by CBS, but it would not have been so dramatic. The exaggeration of the number of offices in the Pentagon by a factor of 6 shows the same kind of bias, as does the implication that CBS had to "find" the Industrial War College lecturers. The criticism of the film, "Roads to the Wall," would have been blunted if CBS had correctly attributed its production to CBS rather than to the Pentagon.

THE ERRORS CBS REFUSES TO ADMIT

The purpose of the CBS reply is not to admit and apologize for errors in *The Selling of the Pentagon*, although that is grudgingly done in a few cases. Rather, CBS set out to show that the critics, not CBS, had erred. Thus the reply is mainly an effort to rebut the numerous criticisms made of the documentary. In addition to the points already discussed, the CBS reply takes up the following criticisms:

(1) The editing of the remarks of Col. John MacNeil, which involved creating a synthetic statement from widely separated sentences in his speech;

(2) The circumstances surrounding the appearance of the Industrial War College lecture team in Peoria, Ill., especially whether or not the visit was arranged by Caterpillar Tractor Co.;

(3) Whether or not the IWC lecturers violated regulations in discussing foreign policy;

(4) The accuracy of the statement that the Pentagon "used" sympathetic Congressmen to interview military heroes such as Maj. James Rowe to counter anti-war reporting;

(5) The charge that CBS used false pretenses to obtain a tape of the interview of Maj. Rowe by Congressman Hébert;

(6) The charge that CBS falsely suggested that the Pentagon spent about $12 million a year on films to be shown to the public;

(7) The charge that CBS gave a misleading impression about a film narrated by Robert Stack;

(8) The charge that CBS implied that an expensive war game was staged for the benefit of a few VIP civilians;

(9) Charges that CBS selectively edited a film of a press briefing by Jerry Friedheim to make it appear that he was unresponsive to newsmen's questions;

(10) ditto for a Saigon news briefing; and

(11) Charges that CBS gave a wrong impression in saying that the U.S. had resumed bombing of North Vietnam.

CBS refuses to admit that there was merit to any of these charges, but in every case its refutation is weak and unconvincing.

(1) CBS justifies creating a synthetic statement and putting it in the mouth of Col. John MacNeil on the ground that each of the sentences used was actually said by Col. MacNeil and their meaning was not altered. It admits that one of the sentences was taken out of chronological order, but it does not mention that this is contrary to the CBS Operating Standards for News and Public Affairs, which state that this kind of transposition must not be done without informing the audience. This rule was adopted in June 1971 after the controversy about The Selling of the Pentagon. But if CBS says that there was nothing wrong with this kind of transposition in *The Selling of the Pentagon*, we wonder how seriously CBS intends to enforce its new regulation.

The same point can be made about the editing of the Henkin interview, which also involved clear violations of the rules against the transposing of answers to questions without giving an indication of this to the audience. In its discussion of the editing of the Henkin interview, CBS makes no mention of the fact that the editing was clearly contrary to the rules later adopted.

These are the most obvious criticisms to be made of the CBS defense of its editing of the MacNeil speech and the Henkin interview. CBS is actually dishonest in suggesting that there was no significance to the fact that it took a sentence out of proper chronological order to begin the synthetic statement it created for Col. MacNeil. The sentence was: "Well, now we're coming to the heart of the problem, Vietnam." This was then followed by a statement the colonel had made about Thailand and two sentences that he had quoted from the Premier of Laos concerning Southeast Asia. The latter two sentences were taken so completely out of context that they were not shown as quotations at all in the CBS synthetic statement.

Why was it necessary to introduce statements about Thailand, Laos, Cambodia and other Southeast Asian countries with the statement on Vietnam which CBS took out of its proper order? CBS did this for the very good reason that it wanted to lead into Col. MacNeil's synthetic statement with this: "The Army has a regulation stating: Personnel should not speak on the foreign policy implications of U.S. involvement in Vietnam." It would appear that CBS wanted to create the impression that Col. MacNeil was speaking in violation of that regulation. The easiest way to do this was to lead off the synthetic statement created for him with a sentence taken out of order. CBS seems not to understand the meaning and importance of context. If it can still say that what it did to Col. MacNeil's statement was fair editing, then no one's words are safe with CBS.

(2) CBS described the National Security Seminar given by the Industrial War College in Peoria, Ill., this way: "The Pentagon has a team of colonels touring the country to lecture on foreign policy. We found them in Peoria, Ill., where they were invited to speak to a mixed audience of civilians and military reservists. The invitation was arranged by Peoria's Caterpillar Tractor Co., which did $39 million of business last year with the Defense Department."

Every one of these sentences was challenged by the critics. The team did not come from the Pentagon, but from the Industrial War College. In addition to colonels, it included a Navy captain and a State Department civilian. The seminars cover 33 topics, including foreign policy, and they are given each year in seven locations throughout the country, primarily for the benefit of military reservists. They were invited to Peoria by the Association of Commerce of Peoria, which shared sponsorship with the 9th Naval District.

CBS, in a lame rejoinder, justifies its phrase, "a team of colonels," by asserting that the Navy captain is equivalent to a colonel and the State Department civilian was a reserve lt. colonel. It does not explain why it called this a "Pentagon" team rather than identifying the responsibility of the Industrial War College (Industrial College of the Armed Forces), but it justifies the misleading term by saying that the military officers are all subject to the authority of the Pentagon. It admits that it should not have said it "found" them in Peoria. It admits that the team lectures on many subjects other than foreign policy, but it defends the misleading statement by saying that the broadcast did not say the team lectured *only* on foreign policy. Presumably if the listeners inferred that, that was their mistake.

CBS says it was justified in saying that Caterpillar arranged the invitation, because an official of Caterpillar was co-chairman of the committee that arranged the seminar and they were told that he and his associates were very helpful "in heading up the committee and making all the necessary arrangements." CBS would apparently have us believe that anything an employee of a company does, including civic activities, can be attributed to the firm that employs him.

(3) CBS accused the lecturers for the Industrial College of the Armed Forces of violating military regulations in discussing foreign policy implications of Vietnam. It was criticized for not pointing out that the talks given by these speakers had been cleared not only by Defense but by the State Department. The Assistant Secretary of Defense says this is all the regulations

require. CBS insists that the talks violated regulations, no matter who cleared them. Since national defense and foreign policy are frequently intertwined, it would seem clear that the Departments of Defense and State are in a better position than CBS to determine whether or not a speech runs counter to government regulations and policy.

(4) CBS was charged with having falsely suggested that friendly Congressmen, specifically Cong. F. Edward Hébert, had been "used" by the Pentagon in broadcasting interviews that they had made with Maj. James Rowe. This was vigorously denied by Cong. Hébert, who denied that the interview with Maj. Rowe was produced at the suggestion of the Pentagon or that the broadcast to his home district involved the use of Pentagon funds. This could easily have been the inference drawn by those who heard the CBS statement. CBS says the program did not say that the Pentagon produced the Hébert-Rowe interview or that it was the Pentagon's idea.

However, it undermines this denial by stressing that Cong. Hébert thanked the colonel who served as liaison with the House Armed Services Committee for bringing Maj. Rowe to him. They do not seem to consider that Cong. Hébert might have asked the colonel to bring Maj. Rowe, who was famous for surviving five years of captivity as a VC prisoner and who successfully escaped, to see him. While denying that it meant to imply what it implied, CBS persists in conveying the same unfair implication.

(5) Cong. Hébert charged that CBS obtained the tape of his interview with Maj. Rowe by telling his office that it wanted it in connection with a documentary it was doing on prisoners of war. CBS denies this, saying that it was public knowledge that it was doing a documentary of public information activities of the Department of Defense at the time it obtained the Hébert tape. CBS asserts that no one on its staff ever represented that the tape it wanted from Cong. Hébert was to be used for a POW documentary.

On the contrary, says CBS, they said they wanted the film in connection with a documentary on Pentagon public relations activities. This is flatly contradicted by Cong. Hébert's press secretary and by the Congressman. Congressman Hébert has put into the record letters or memos from the offices of five other congressmen who assert that they were approached by the same CBS staffers who approached Congresman Hébert's office to obtain tapes of interviews with Maj. Rowe. Four of them said they were told that CBS wanted these tapes in connection with a documentary it was doing on POW's. CBS makes no mention of this evidence confirming Cong. Hébert's charge that the CBS staff sought tapes of interviews between congressmen and Maj .Rowe under the pretense that they were working on a documentary on POW's. In a delightful evasion, CBS says:

"Months after the Rowe-Hébert program was delivered to Mr. Seabrooks, Mr. Branon contacted Mr. Hébert's office and the offices of other Representatives to obtain information with respect to additional Congressional interviews with Major Rowe and other military personnel, including other former prisoners of war. It is at this point, seemingly, that the confusion began. The focus on additional Rowe interviews and other POW interviews may well have been the genesis of the misunderstanding which arose."

We are expected to believe that five Congressional offices all got the impression that CBS wanted these tapes in connection with a documentary on POW's even though they were all presumably told that CBS wanted them in connection with a documentary on Defense Department public relations activities. That is too strange a coincidence to be swallowed.

(6) CBS devoted nearly one-fourth of "The Selling of the Pentagon" to films made by the military and available to the public. It said that most of the films were made originally for troop information but a large number was later released for public showing. It said that the Pentagon spends over $12 million a year on films. Later, in criticizing anticommunist films made by the Pentagon, CBS said: "But to the filmmakers at the Pentagon, with at least $12 million a year to spend, 1946 seems to have lasted a whole generation." One could easily infer from these statements that a very large part of the $12 million goes for films that are intended for public release. The Pentagon notes that the great bulk of the films are made for troop training, research development, recruiting, medical and religious use. It charges that CBS was wrong in implying that the $12 million in films was largely used to influence the public. CBS responds that it had no intention of implying that most of the viewers probably inferred from what was said.

(7) It is charged that CBS showed Robert Stack narrating a Defense Department film in a way that suggested that he was doing a film on the use of weapons in Vietnam when, in fact, the film was about unarmed reconnaissance pilots. The brief film clip used by CBS did give the impression that Stack was going to talk about guns in Vietnam. CBS says they had no intention of implying this and that "no such implication was created." Nevertheless, the inference was created.

(8) "The Selling of the Pentagon" gave many viewers the impression that a large military training exercise called "Brass Strike" was put on for the benefit of a small group of civilian VIP's. Describing this military exercise, CBS said: "An air and land assault on enemy territory was simulated for the visitors." The Defense Department points out that the training exercise would have taken place with or without the VIP visitors and that many other observers, including military personnel saw it. The answer CBS gives is that it did not say that the exercise would not have taken place in the absence of the VIP visitors, that it was other than a training exercise and that no other observers were present. True, CBS did not say any of those things, it only created that implication.

(9) It was charged that CBS showed Assistant Secretary of Defense Jerry Friedheim declining to answer half of the questions he was asked at a press briefing when actually at that briefing he responded to 31 of the 34 questions asked. The complaint was that CBS deliberately focused on those

questions that Mr. Friedheim declined to answer for security reasons to create the impression that he did not provide the press with much information. It was charged that CBS used the same technique to indicate that press briefings in Saigon were characterized by "no comment" answers to newsmens' questions.

CBS said that at the Friedheim briefing at least 56 questions were asked and Mr. Friedheim was unable to answer 11 of these completely for varying reasons. This meant that he answered 80 per cent of the questions asked completely. CBS showed six questions being asked, the first three of which Mr. Friedman declined to answer or could not answer. In the CBS portrayal, his response rate was only 50 per cent compared with the actual 80 per cent which CBS says prevailed for the entrie briefing. CBS says: "This is a fair representation which does not reflect adversely on Mr. Friedheim." What CBS selected to show was clearly not typical of Mr. Friedheim's performance at the briefing. CBS appeared to be trying to make the point that the press briefings are an occasion when the press is trying, without much success, to extract information from unwilling Defense Department spokesmen.

In introducing Mr. Friedheim, CBS described him as an "adversary" of the press. The briefing was described as a "confrontation," and CBS said of Mr. Friedheim: "He does not, of course, tell all he knows; he wouldn't have his job long if he did." There followed the carefully selected segment from the briefing showing Mr. Friedheim avoiding answering reporters' questions. That is what CBS calls a "fair" representation. The same kind of treatment was given the press briefing in Saigon for exactly the same reason. CBS said the daily press briefing there was "known among newsmen in Saigon as the Five O'Clock Follies." It indicated that the most popular phrase at the briefing was "no comment."

It then illustrated this by showing a film clip of the briefer declining to answer questions. The Defense Department claims that this was not a typical scene. CBS does not deny that the sequence it showed was not typical. Instead it argues that the briefer should have been authorized to answer the particular questions that he was shown declining to answer. Arguable though that may be, it does not get CBS off the hook for presenting an atypical sequence and passing it off to the viewers as completely representative of the daily briefings.

(10) CBS was criticized for saying that the phrase "protective reaction" means that the U.S. resumed the bombing of North Vietnam. The Defense Department states that "protective reaction" means a very limited kind of bombing undertaken to protect unarmed reconnaissance flights over North Vietnam. It emphasizes that this does not mean the resumption of the widespread bombing of North Vietnam carried out prior to November 1968. CBS responds that it only said the bombing had resumed, without saying that large scale bombing had been resumed. They say that the Defense Department has made it clear that "protective reaction" bombing is different from

this kind, and many in the audience could well have been misled into thinking that the phrase, "the U.S. resumed the bombing of North Vietnam" meant
that the U.S. had resumed the kind of bombing that was being carried out in
1968.

THE QUESTION CBS DID NOT EVEN TRY TO ANSWER

Although CBS once claimed to have an answer for every one of the
criticisms of "The Selling of the Pentagon," its comprehensive reply to the
critics leaves many questions unanswered. AIM criticized 23 points in the
CBS documentary, and CBS dealt with only 13 of these in its "comprehensive" reply. Ten points, with 35 questions attached, were completely ignored.

Among the questions CBS avoided were these: (1) was it not inaccurate
and unfair to suggest that John Wayne narrated Defense Department films
in return for help in making "The Green Berets"? (2) How does CBS define
its phrase, "Pentagon propaganda," and would any factual description of
the record of communist oppression be labeled "propaganda" by CBS? Does
CBS know that Walter Cronkite has changed his mind about the aggressive
nature of communism, and if not why was it implied that he had changed
his views?

In analyzing Pentagon films, why did CBS focus on films on communism and then complain that they dealt with communism? How does CBS
reconcile its assertion that we adopted a policy of "peaceful coexistence"
prior to 1961 with the Bay of Pigs invasion, the Cuban missile crisis, the
building of the Berlin Wall and the Gulf of Tonkin resolution?

Many of the questions CBS did not try to answer probed the most
serious flaw in "The Selling of the Pentagon," the fact that it was fundamentally dishonest. CBS says no one has refuted the basic veracity of the
documentary. That is precisely what AIM did. That is why CBS has not answered AIM's deep probing questions.

Mr. Speaker, if anyone is further interested in the type of propaganda,
such as was evidenced by the "Selling of the Pentagon" program, I add this
bit of information from Claude Witze's column in Air Force magazine:

[From Air Force magazine, February 1972]

In case anyone is still interested, "The Selling of the Pentagon" is
available for rental. It can be obtained for a fee of $65 from American Docu-
mentary Films, a nonprofit educational organization with offices at 336 West
84th St., New York, N.Y. 10024, or from 379 Bay St., San Francisco, Calif.

American Documentary Films advertises that it circulates "Films for
Agitation." In addition to the CBS masterpiece, you can select from a list that
includes, for example, "79 Springtimes," described as "a brilliant impres-
sionist biographical tribute to Ho Chi Minh." And there is "Hanoi, Martes
13," which is a "moving salute to the Vietnamese," presumably those in North
Vietnam. Then there is available, "Stagolee: Bobby Seale in Prison," a film

in which the Panther leader speaks out, and another picture in which Angela Davis tells it like it is, from her viewpoint in jail.

The American Documentary Film catalog does not include "Road to the Wall," a documentary produced by CBS for the Department of Defense in 1962.

The following article, by Representative Lionel Van Deerlin of California, is reprinted in its entirety from the Congressional Record *for Thursday, June 15, 1972.*

Mr. Speaker, fundamental constitutional rights are an issue of primary concern to all Americans. Governmental regulation of the news media is fundamentally improper, under our system.

Our colleague, FRED ROONEY, has touched on some critical points in an address delivered May 23 to the Pennsylvania Broadcasters Association. Mr. ROONEY's thoughtful remarks provide considerable background and guidance in this sensitive area.

The text of his speech follows:

OPENING REMARKS ON NEED TO EDUCATE MEMBERS OF CONGRESS "IN THE CLEAREST AND SIMPLEST WAY POSSIBLE ON THE MAJOR MATTERS WHICH CONCERN YOU AS BROADCASTERS"

There's an interesting cover story in this month's issue of "Nation's Business," which I am sure you have all seen.

The opening sentence of the story poses a perplexing question:

"How would you like to own a business where you are required every three years to justify your performance to seven political appointees and perhaps lose that business if they don't think you measure up?"

I'd say that's a unique kind of business.

I'm sure it occurs to you when you fill out your license renewal applications.

You've always been beholden to government for your broadcast franchise, and subject to Federal controls and laws.

But lately, you're being made more aware than ever before.

For many years the license renewal policy of the FCC was consistent.

The Commission, in reviewing renewal applications gave great weight to the past performance of a licensee on the reasonable assumption that proven record of good performance was better evidence of future quality performance than any other measurable factor.

Now, because of recent court decisions, any individual or group can challenge a station's right to continue operating.

The station is compelled to respond, no matter how unrealistic the complaint.

And a recent decision by the U.S. Court of Appeals in Washington has raised concern that a broadcaster might be required to pay for all expenses incurred by the challenger, even after meeting his demands.

Such license challenges have put more than 100 stations under attack, and two owners out of business.

The final solution to the license renewal matter, in my view, is to be found in the Congress.

We will have a permanent national renewal policy, binding on both the FCC and the courts, only when specific criteria are written into law.

Nearly 200 Members of Congress in both Houses and in both parties have lent their names to renewal legislation.

Nearly 100 bills are pending.

My bill, H.R. 13193, would extend the license period to 5 years for radio stations and retain the 3-year statutory limitation for television stations.

At the same time it would assure both that their licenses would be renewed if the station could show the FCC a good-faith effort to serve the needs and interests of its community during the preceding license period.

The public interest requires that the broadcast industry be a stable one in which licensees whose past record of performance meets or exceeds broadcast criteria established by the FCC have a reasonable degree of assurance that their applications for license renewals will be determined upon such criteria, and not some extraneous issues not directly related to the quality of service extended to their broadcast area.

My bill does this, without in any way eliminating any existing rights enjoyed by those who desire to contest a license application or otherwise bring to the attention of the FCC any alleged failures of a licensee.

Unfortunately, you are not going to get license renewal legislation in this, the 92nd Congress, but the issue is still very much alive.

I urge all broadcasters to use the next 8 or 9 months to educate their Congressmen as to the need for this legislation.

Permit me also to call your attention to legislation which I have introduced in the House with some 25 cosponsors to remove existing Federal legal barriers to the broadcasting of information about the Pennsylvania lottery.

All news media in Pennsylvania and other States which have implemented state-operated lotteries have encountered the restrictions imposed by Federal anti-lottery laws.

These Federal laws involve interstate commerce, use of the mails and broadcasting.

A number of related bills are pending in several House committees. Only mine, however, has tied all the necessary revisions of Federal law into a single legislative package which now is before the House Judiciary Subcommittee No. 2.

That subcommittee seems almost equally divided on the question of removing Federal obstacles to the State-operated lotteries.

I have been advised, for example, that the subcommittee's two members from the State of California, Congressman Waldie and Danielson have indicated they oppose these measures.

On the other hand, there have been recent reports that California is looking at the east coast State lotteries with considerable interest.

Obviously, if California establishes its own lottery, then that State's broadcasters will be in the same shoes in which Pennsylvania broadcasters find themselves now.

Here, then, is an opportunity for your group to contact your affiliates in California and seek their help to win the support of the two California Congressmen on the Judiciary Subcommittee No. 2 for favorable action on the lottery legislation.

In addition to license renewal problems, the broadcast industry now has to face the Federal Trade Commission's recent counter-advertising proposal which, if enacted, has the potential of undermining and destroying the entire financial base of commercial broadcasting.

The concept of counter-advertising is so broad in scope as to cover most products and services now advertised over your stations.

I know from experience that no more consumer-oriented groups exist than my constituency.

And I also know that no company is going to pay to advertise its product on radio and television if by doing so it will automatically give a right to someone else to attack it on the same station.

The broadcasters' plight is of concern to all American business, because if counter-advertising comes, it's only a short step to the point at which any form of advertising would be affected.

If your industry can be undermined by Government policy, so can other industries.

Counter-advertising and license challenges may head your current inventory of headaches.

But you've been attacked in the name of public interest in a lot of other ways.

There's been a ban on broadcast advertising of lawful products whose advertising is permitted in all other media.

That only cost you $200 million a year in cigarette revenue—and now there's a lot of Government interest in your proprietary drug advertising.

There's been the prime-time access rule.

That's only depriving you of about 600 hours of network programing a year and a drop-off in audience between 7:30 and 8 p.m.

I understand there was a well-intentioned reason for the rule, but like so many of the well-intentioned regulations you're working with today, it hasn't worked.

It has, however, given rise to other ideas for controlling program content by times of day and segments of the audience, and encouraging parents agitating for all kinds of innovations in children's programs—like totally eliminating commercials.

There is for this election year, a new political-spending bill.

I don't know how you're going to fare on that.

I do know that the equal time provision—section 315 of the communications act—is still in force, making fun situations for comedian Pat Paulsen, but depriving the American voter of television encounters between the major presidential candidates, in the words of Frank Stanton, "crippling the most constructive use of broadcasting in the electoral process."

There's more, of course.

Any number of tortured applications of the fairness doctrine.

Compulsory access to the air stripping you of the responsibility for what you broadcast even though you're still held accountable for it.

The constant threat of investigation that hangs over your head and yours alone among the media.

The pressures on broadcast news which are a part of this.

The uncertainty as you approach license renewal time that regardless of how conscientiously you've tried to serve your community, you still may find yourself in a contest with special interest groups who want to take your license for any of a growing number of reasons.

And now some icing on the cake—the Justice Department antitrust suits against the networks contesting their program production, acquisition and sales practices.

I think the suits are way off base.

I think they are against the public interest.

I think they will fail.

And I think they are just another indication—as many of your new problems are—of an administration trying desperately to keep broadcasting off balance and bend it to its own end.

The public interest can be served best if we put the roles of government and the press in proper perspective.

Government is an institution, and so is the press.

Our founding fathers wisely foresaw that these two institutions would, in most cases, be adversaries and seldom, if ever, allies.

It is the responsibility of government to govern.

It is the responsibility of the press to report how government is functioning.

Both must ultimately account to the public.

When your industry is encroached upon by government, the public suffers.

The attack began in Des Moines in November, 1969, with a lecture from Spiro Agnew on network news bias and how the networks must be made more responsive to the views of the people.

Some of his rhetoric may have seemed amusing—even appropriate —to you at the time, but it just might have been the first step toward dividing and conquering your industry by intimidating your news people and by dampening your enthusiasm to speak out on matters of national and local importance.

Senator Bob Dole then took up the fight and flew around the countryside assailing the "liberal media".

And the President's closest staff assistants are lately growing more vocal.

H. R. Haldeman was a guest on the "Today" program several months ago.

He took that opportunity to deliver a salvo at the credibility of the news media and at what he believes to be television's continuing anti-administration bias.

James Keogh, chief of research and writing for Richard Nixon during the 1968 election campaign, and later a special assistant to the President, is out with a new book titled "President Nixon and the Press."

It details the President's poor treatment by the media.

Mr. Keogh also spoke about it in a recent "Today" program interview.

And earlier this month, on a public broadcast service program, White House speechwriter Patrick Buchanan bluntly suggested that because CBS and NBC are biased in their news coverage, along with some publications, the administration might be obliged to sponsor antitrust action to break up their "monopoly" on ideas.

He also said that the current Justice Department suits against network programing are "just testing out the theory."

The Justice Department quickly denied this, and Senator Dole promptly and officially added his disagreement with Buchanan.

Of course, Mr. Buchanan said that he was expressing his personal opinion.

All the administration people do that, including Mr. Agnew.

Then try to be careful not to give the impression of a massive frontal assault.

For instance, Mr. Buchanan pointedly excluded ABC from his news antitrust wishes.

White House communications chief Herb Klein salutes your freedom of broadcasting rights every chance he gets after someone else in the administration has scolded you.

And you will get messages from the President at your big conventions about the great job you *station people* are doing.

Just to keep you a little more off balance, and possibly undecided about what's going on, Clay Whitehead, the administration's spokesman on communications policy, tells you the things you really like to hear—about the deregulation of radio, and after that, gee, maybe television.

About his opposition to the FCC's banning newspaper-CATV cross-ownership in the same market, and the present rule prohibiting crossownership of TV stations and cable systems.

He also tells you about the administration's great disturbance at the way the trend is going in connection with FCC and court rulings on access and the fairness doctrine.

A few weeks ago he even went on new ground and asked the Nation's newspaper publishers to oppose, with him, a trend in Government to stifle freedom of the press.

And he called the fairness doctrine "a runaway theory" that may trample newspapers next.

Mr. Whitehead is a regular Paul Revere.

I agree with his warnings and nearly everything he says.

But I don't think he voices the true feelings of the present administration.

The name of the administration game is quiet intimidation and the encouragement of splits in your industry between stations and their networks.

There's a fast thrust at an annoyance of the movement and then a denial of restrictive intent; an occasional subpoena and investigation and then a pat on the head.

When caught with a hot potato, like the ITT mess or a war going badly for all to see on the evening news, there's always an antitrust action, or the threat of one to take the heat off.

There is supposed to be liberal bias in television news.

The Nixon administration has told us this right along.

The networks are said to freeze out opposing points of view and opposing information.

Let's look at the freeze.

President Nixon on 29 occasions since his inaugural has taken over the networks for a "major" pronouncement, or one so advertised.

It could be every month if he wanted.

He has held a number, a dwindling number, of televised news conferences and several "conversations" with network interviewers.

He has appeared in fragments of innumerable news broadcasts—this above and beyond all the coverage granted Vice President Agnew, various cabinet members and other Republican dignitaries.

Even the President's staff men are promoting their books and their views on the tube.

And since the present administration does make our nation's policy, does keep the records, does appoint, hire and fire people, it does supply a vast amount of news and views, all duly reported on a daily basis.

I hope a Democratic administration is so lucky next year.

The question to be asked, of course, is what does the public think?

What bias does it see on television?

Earlier this year TV Guide took the trouble to find out.

It commissioned Opinion Research Corporation to sample viewer attitudes on TV news credibility around the country.

The findings were highly interesting.

A majority of Americans think television offers the most complete political coverage of any news medium.

Most consider television fairest and most objective of the media and see little difference in fairness between each of the networks.

Perhaps most significant, where it is believed television news bias exists, opinions divided almost 50–50 on alleged favoritism:

A quarter of those interviewed see a pro-Nixon bias; another quarter see an anti-Nixon bias; 12 percent think the Republicans are treated more kindly; 13 percent think the Democrats are; 16 percent maintain that liberals get better treatment; 14 percent are sure conservatives do.

Those are pretty good marks, pretty balanced opinion, and most of those interviewed didn't detect bias of any kind.

What turned up in the study in fact confirms the findings of other continuing surveys of public attitudes toward TV news over the last decade.

I can understand why many broadcasters—faced with the spectrum of counter-advertising, meeting license renewal challenges and trying to interpret the conflicting decisions made under the umbrella of the fairness doctrine—feel like the "shuttlecock in a badminton game."

Don't take these blows at your freedoms or at your economic base.

Fight back.

Tell your story to the public—the story of a great free and competitive industry, unexcelled anywhere in the world—an industry which brings all Americans everything from wholesome entertainment and up-to-the-minute news in their homes and their cars to live pictures from China and the moon.

Tell your story in terms of the new products and services developed by American business which, through broadcast advertising, can be sold all over the Nation, providing for the American people the goods and services they want at prices kept as low as possible because they can be mass produced and sold.

You have an honest and honorable story to tell—a story that needs to be told to the public and to the Congress.

Only you can tell it.

The time to begin is now.